- by -

Michael A. Aquino, Ph.D.
Lt. Colonel, Psychological Operations (Ret.)
United States Army

ISBN-13:
978-1544178424

ISBN-10:
1544178425

Books by Michael A. Aquino

[all available in both printed and Kindle ebook editions]

Non-Fiction

The Church of Satan (2 Volumes)
Extreme Prejudice:
    The Presidio "Satanic Abuse" Scam
IlluminAnX: Rosicrucianism Reawakened
<u>The MindWar Trilogy</u>
    MindWar
    MindStar
    FindFar
The Neutron Bomb
The Temple of Set (2 Volumes)

Fiction

FireForce: A Star Wars *Parody*
    Including: Secret of the Lost Ark
Morlindalë: Song of Illuminate Darkness
    - by "The One Ring"
Ode to Esmé: Memoirs of Captain Nemo
We Break the Sword: The Nazi Peace of 1940

Autobiographical

Ghost Rides
    Including: *Grail Mission*

Edited

Pegasus in Pinfeathers: Collected Poems 1919-1928
    - by Betty Ford

Dedicated To

Janet F. Aquino
Scarborough Fair

About halfway between West Egg and New York, the motor road hastily joins the railroad and runs beside it for a quarter of a mile, so as to shrink away from a certain desolate area of land.

This is a valley of ashes - a fantastic farm where ashes grow like wheat into ridges, hills, and grotesque gardens; where ashes take the form of houses and chimneys and rising smoke; and finally, with a transcendent effort, of men who move dimly and already-crumbling through the powdery air.

Occasionally a line of grey cars crawls along an invisible track, gives out a ghastly creak, and comes to rest; and immediately the ash-grey men swarm up with leaden spades and stir up an impenetrable cloud which screens their obscure operations from sight.

Above the grey land and the spasms of bleak dust which drift endlessly over it repose the eyes of Dr. T.J. Eckleburg: blue and gigantic - their retinas a yard high. They stare out from no face, but instead from a pair of enormous yellow spectacles which pass over an invisible nose. Evidently some obscure oculist set them there before sinking himself into eternal blindness, or merely forgetting them and moving away. But his eyes, dimmed a little by many days under the sun and rain, brood on enigmatically over the spectral landscape.

- F. Scott Fitzgerald
The Great Gatsby, 1925

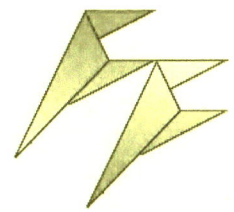

Table of Contents

Preface

> In recent years nuclear physicists have discovered a strange world of subatomic particles, fragments of atoms smaller than the imagination can picture, fragments of materials which do not obey the laws of gravity. Antimatter composed of inside-out material, shadow-matter that can penetrate ten miles of lead shielding. Hidden deep in the heart of strange new elements are secrets beyond human understanding - new powers, new dimensions, worlds within worlds, unknown ...
> - The Control Voice
> "The Production and Decay of Strange Particles"
> *The Outer Limits*, April 20, 1964

In 2013 the strange particle *MindWar* was published. Instead of decaying, however, it has emitted two even stranger particles: *MindStar* (2016) and now *FindFar* (2017). Altogether these three particles meld to generate an *über*strange trimolecule, exposure to which resynapsizes the human brain to regard the existential phenomenon of sentient humanity in radically-new manifestations.

MindWar is a practical manual for the retirement of traditional, physical warfare (PhysWar/PW) in favor of cooperative, pacific invention against an artificially-controlled environmental atmosphere subconsciously aligning the cognitive processes of the human brain away from natural chaos to supernatural serenity.

MindStar addresses the one component of human mentality that the externalized *MindWar* intentionally postpones: the metaphysical "soul", or more precisely eightfold emanations collectively comprising the MindStar of eternal, immortal, isolate self-consciousness.

O.K., so that was the easy part.

Aficionados of MW will [p]recall that a successful MW campaign requires first the designing, then the gradual implementation of an improved entity profile: either the "best practical" *áristos* or, in ideal opportunities, the perfected *polis* of *kalokagathia*. This analysis involves forecasting, but once again not what conventionally passes for forecasting: static "snapshots" of estimated future points in linear time.

Instead MW utilizes a Fourth-Dimensional, dynamic calculus called **FindFar** (FF), which is the subject of this third book in the series.

FF is not a static picture but one in motion: a projection which is in constant harmonization with the MW campaign during its activation. Indeed there is a "double-dynamic" in process, since the targeted future and the current standpoint-of-perspective are both changing relative to each other, and both against any external "backdrops": a continuum of **true**, not Einsteinian-absurd relativity.

The task of *FindFar* is not just to describe this machinery, but to do so without bewildering the reader. Any tool, no matter how elegant, is useless unless one knows how to use it reasonably effortlessly. Hence *FF* is written not so much as a turgid textbook as a conversation, interacting with the reader and frequently going back over obscure or complex points. The result, I hope, will be a reading experience as stimulating as it is informative.

In places I daresay it is also sobering. MW is not a pleasant puzzle for ivory-tower entertainment; it is an instrument of power and force to overcome the formidable inertia of an existing global crisis of intolerable destruction, misery, pain, and death. MW's application requires not just understanding and wisdom, but the clearsighted coldness and divine detachment of Dr. T.J. Eckleburg. There will be ample flexibility for pleasure once the bloodflow of PW has been arrested.

If you eventually find yourself in an opportune position to activate MW in whole or part, FF should be a practical resource. Short of such an opportunity, it may also be of value as a stand-alone tool, replacing the clumsiness and obsolescence of conventional forecasting with a sleeker, swifter alternative. So take it out on a test-drive and let me know how well it works for you.

Learn to smile.

San Francisco
February 2, 2017 CE

Chapter 1: FINDing the FAR Future

Change is the law of life. And those who look only to
the past or present are certain to miss the future.
                                        - John F. Kennedy

The future belongs to those who believe in the
beauty of their dreams.
                                        - Eleanor Roosevelt

A. *Status Quo*: Chaos

1. "Frozen in the Headlights"

Right out of the starting gate, conventional
approaches to political problem-solving are doomed to
confusion, frustration, and failure for a very simple
reason: **There is no framework for solution and
phased implementation.**

Rather the subject problem is treated as an
amorphous, discrete incident or state-of-affairs;
accordingly any proposed "solutions" are designed and
considered for immediate appeasement and gratification
of [preferred] interested parties.

The **symptoms** - **not** the causes - are treated, and
"the can is kicked down the road" - only to reappear
thereupon at a later date, most probably in an even more
problematic state.

2. Three Headlights

There are three primary reasons for this, as well as numerous subsets of the three. They are:

a. Pressure

In a world of political nation/states, national governments are expected to be the initiators and agents of problem solution. With few exceptions these governments are short-tenured, dependent upon formal elections or factional/popular support to remain in authority. They are accordingly under constant pressure for immediate, not long-term solutions to perceived national or international problems.

The usual response is to look for a showpiece of immediate gratification rather than the frustration of an extended policy that may actually be more practical.

A conspicuous contemporary example is the concern about "global warming". While there is scientific uncertainty about how much, if any of this is the fault of human contamination of the Earth's atmosphere, as opposed, for instance, to subtle changes in Solar activity and/or Earth's orbital path/tilt, the possibility that there might actually be nothing completely arresting or reversing which humans can do about the trend is too fearsome and fatalistic to confront; so the Solar/orbital explanations are ignored and a scapegoat sought with a neck to wring, in this case that of the fossil-fuel industry. Shut it down; save the Earth.

The result: impulsive protests, pickets, boycotts, riots until there is some governmental response to assuage the fear. But because of that pressure such response will necessarily be more cosmetic, placating, immediately-gratifying than substantive.

b. Ulterior Motives

Alternately the issue is not really excoriated for itself, but as one of a number of means for the ambitious and disaffected to unseat the existing government for its alleged helplessness and ineptitude. The replacement regime may have no better solution in mind, other than trying to divert public attention from the scarecrow once it is in power.

In 1960 Democratic Presidential candidate John F. Kennedy and his party raised the spectre of a "missile gap" with the Soviet Union. Since both superpowers already possessed the nuclear weaponry to obliterate each other [not to mention the rest of the planet] several times over, this monster-under-the-bed rather begged the question, but no matter: Elect Jack and he'd zap the gap.

c. No Way Out

Or, and least confrontably, of course, there may simply be **no** possible or practical solution: Global warming may in truth be caused by conditions completely beyond human control, and political instability and agitation is actually, ultimately emotional denial and apocalyptic panic.

3. Thousand-Pound Canaries

Nor is there any paucity of supernational problems to worry the world above and beyond international and intranational conflicts. In addition to the aforementioned global warming concern, the United Nations identifies the planet's principal problems [alphabetized, not prioritized].

And yes, this is a **bummer** of a long list:

a. Africa

It is Africa's fortune to be the most ancient and magical of continents, and misfortune to have a history of unparalleled suffering, often ignored by the rest of the world, and still a scourge today. Wars and catastrophes that would be shocking elsewhere pass in the night, unnoticed there. A new respect and compassion is long overdue for this cradle of human civilization.

b. Aging

There are a relative few cultures that are advanced enough to respect, love, and care for their elders. In many more their fate is a lonely, neglected, and miserable one. At issue here is humanity's regard for its own creation and lineage, which must be relearned as much from the great civilizations of antiquity as restored in a future utopia.

c. Agriculture

While science has discovered much about the life of *flora* & *fauna*, it has not been as successful in learning consideration for them and a balance in husbandry amidst the Earth's still-fertile areas. High standards are demanded beyond national borders if Gaia is to survive and nurture her children.

d. AIDS

Many of humanity's curses are the result of natural hazard and universal entropy. AIDS is quite different: a scourge that we have brought upon ourselves, and which should never have been allowed to survive, much less grow these many years. Exceptional, uncommon effort must be made to send it back into nonexistence.

e. Atomic Energy

From the myths of the ancients to the scholasticism of the medievals, it was axiomatic that the universe is everywhere subject to Natural Law, also known as the gods or God, which is breached by mankind at its peril. In daring to smash the atom, we let loose, in the words of J. Robert Oppenheimer, "Death the Destroyer of Worlds". At once the least-noticed and most-final of all these challenges and dangers, it is as imminent as the clock-hands on the *Bulletin of the Atomic Scientists.*

f. Children

As shameful as the world's treatment of its elderly is its carelessness concerning its young, the more so in an age where the comfort of family has all too often been replaced by the distance and disinterest of alienation, foreshadowing the plight of the old at the end of the same journey.

g. Decolonization

The enslavement of entire nations by their fellows should have become extinct long ago, yet vestiges still linger to this day, often in economic guise.

h. Demining

Numerous local PhysWars have come and gone, but their land mines and other unexploded ordinance remain, maiming or killing farmers or children who pick up such "toys".

i. Democracy

"The worst possible form of government except for the alternatives." Plato was right to dread the *eikasia* of the masses; if democracy is to succeed, the electorate must be diligently schooled in its wise application.

j. Development

It was once fashionable to assume that the poorest and most desperate countries of the post-colonial "Third World" would raise themselves up to the affluent and leisured lifestyles of their old conquerors. Rarely has this happened; the excesses of the centuries of extractions need to be remedied just as enduringly.

k. Disarmament

It is not just atomic weaponry that poses a danger to humanity; the proliferation of conventional armaments is proving every bit as lethal - and, unlike nukes, is everywhere in PhysWar use.

l. Environment

The ecosphere in all its aspects suffers from pollution, contamination, and outright destruction: endangering not just humanity but many other species of life as well.

m. Family

Pressures of PhysWar, economic hardship, and social stresses threaten the safety and comfort of the family unit, with painful consequences to husbands, wives, and children. This relates also to the specific plights of children and the aged.

n. Food

The adequacy, safety, quality, and equitable availability and distribution of nutrition worldwide. "Unprofitable" excesses in production are routinely discarded while, far away and unnoticed, children and their parents starve slowly to death.

o. Governance

The prudent creation and maintenance of national governmental structures and systems that benefit their citizenry and sustain the resources of their territories. Whatever ideology clothes this effort is not nearly as important as its effectiveness and humanitarian benefit.

p. Health

Prevention and treatment of disease and injury, accessible to the poor as well as the wealthy. Unceasing vigilance over living environmental conditions to ensure they do not threaten the health of the living.

q. Human Rights

Above social-contractual civil rights particular to each nation are human rights of life, liberty, and dignity which all beings should enjoy - but rarely do.

r. Human Settlement

As all the habitable areas of the planet have been found and claimed by nation-states, and as none of them has any population control or resource-sharing programs sufficient for balance, overcrowded cities, slums, and ghettos continue to proliferate: breeding-grounds for many of these other critical problems.

s. Humanitarian Assistance

Natural disasters and human PhysWars periodically devastate areas of the planet, requiring prompt and adequate emergency aid beyond the capacity of the local government(s).

t. International Law

Always problematic, because there is rarely international agreement on laws beyond those of individual states, nor effective policing and enforcement resources for such covenants as are agreed to.

u. Oceans

The Earth is an ocean-planet, interrupted by a relative few, comparatively small land masses. Humans forget this truth at their peril. If the oceans die, the planet dies, regardless what purely-land efforts are made.

v. Peace & Security

The unpleasant truth of PhysWar is that, while everywhere rhetorically denounced, it has come to be the economic and industrial backbone of humanity. MW insists that this need not and should not be so.

w. Persons with Disabilities

Further aggravating and complicating the issues of health, children, family, and aging. personal illness, incapacity, and weakness jeopardize not only the individual afflicted, but supportive friends, relatives, and social services as well.

x. Population

Human reproduction is everywhere explosive and completely uncontrolled, resulting in the overrunning of resources, irreversible contamination, extinction of nonhuman life, and extreme suffering among the increasingly-overcrowded. Attempts to control this epidemic are howled down as discrimination, racism, genocide, xenophobia. Very simply, if it is not brought under control - if it is even still possible to do so - it alone will terminally unbalance the Earth's ecosphere.

y. Refugees

As countries and regions become inhospitable and uninhabitable from natural disasters, PhysWar, or climate change, their original inhabitants will leave in search of survival elsewhere. The "elsewheres" are, however, already populated and resource-allocated. Worse yet, this problem promises to increase on a compound basis as it interacts with overpopulation.

z. Terrorism

When desperate, deprived, and angry people cannot get the life-support and benefits they feel they deserve by cooperation, they will attempt to seize them by force and violence, including by the disruption and if necessary destruction of national social orders.

aa.   Volunteerism

While many charitable individuals and groups are willing to do what they can to alleviate some or all of these global problems, such humanitarians rarely enjoy the funding and backing they need; and even face obstruction and injury themselves from those who profit from the existing PhysWars and other miseries.

ab.   Water

The "common denominator" of the majority of these global issues, from oceans to populations. Clean, clear, pure water is the substance of all Earthly life. Whenever it is contaminated, reduced, or eliminated, the Earth dies a little more.

ac. Women

In a world everywhere dominated by PhysWar violence and its societal reflections, women, whose reproductive bodies and biologies make them more vulnerable to and dependent upon males not so limited, everywhere suffer discrimination, marginalization, and exploitation. Their human dignity demands respect equal to males', and indeed extra consideration in keeping with their additional needs as the bringers and nurturers of life.

4. Starfish

Altogether this overwhelming, daunting list certainly starts ourselves, MindWar, and this book out glumly. Let us suppose that MW can be activated to solve a governmental or border crisis in the Ukraine. With all of the above megaproblems still crippling that geography and its surrounds, is such modest success worth the time, effort, and expense? Or is it rather the proverbial "drop in the bucket"?

In answer MW invokes the parable of the starfish washed up on the shore. A compassionate beachcomber notices it and places it gently back into the sea to live instead of die. Has this small act meant anything for the Earth as a planet? Perhaps not, but it's meant something to that little starfish.

So MW is in the starfish-rescue business, saving not everything but **something**, where and when it can. **That's** the justification for the *MindWar* book, and now this one in supplement to it.

5. Activation

The first step in actually, rather than cosmetically solving posed problems is the development and application of a framework for both analysis and corrective practical implementation.

Such a framework first identifies the problem's components, then fixes the problem by addressing them, and - just as importantly - scheduling the fix progressively against future benchmarks. So it is an analysis with both a *status quo* (the situation at present) and a *status post* (the situation after the fix, at a projected future date).

6. Law

a. Definition

A descriptive law is a statement of exclusive, invariable cause-and-effect.

This statement does not extend to the "how" or the "why" of the process.

b. Classification

In his *Summa Theologica* St. Thomas Aquinas (1225-74) described the ordering of the universe by four types of law, detailed below. Do **not** make the common mistake of assuming that only Human Law is relevant to contemporary conflict-resolution. The other three are just as present today as in Aquinas' era, and if anything even more forceful.

Both Eternal and Natural Law are present in the 95% "pattern thinking" of subconsciousness, which is why they are omnipresent and preemptive of the others.

Divine Law is a hybrid: It is "announced" in the 5% of consciousness, but is assimilated into the 95% subconscious once accepted. Accordingly Divine Law is at once the easiest of the three subconscious Laws for the MWarrior to control, and in many instances an absolutely crucial preemption. Contemporarily, for instance, both Israel and the Islamic State [to name just two of many examples] are driven by what they believe to be the realities and commandments of their gods, with their self-constructed (Human) laws and practices in compliance with and obedience to that Divine Law perception. This is exactly why third-party countries or mediators fail: They ignore the [permanent] 95% and waste their time in exhaustive, futile, and temporary 5%.

(1) Eternal Law

Aquinas, in keeping with the idiom of the Catholic Church, saw the entirety of the universe as the creation and continuation of the mind and will of God, which by assumption is above and beyond human comprehension. All that can be known about it is that it **is**, because there is existence of things and their behaviors, not absence.

This theory, however, requires the arbitrary presumption of time being both linear and finite [cf. Chapter #2], with the universe having a moment of creation as well as one termination, between which is a single, universally-interrelated timeline. In short [or in this case long], creation requires a creator; destruction a destroyer. Within Christian ideology this concept is known as **eschatology**, especially emphasizing its conclusion.

Internally the difficulty with this concept is that it necessarily raises the question of priority: If only God existed prior to creation, how could he know/distinguish himself, or **conceive** creation? Is it possible for there to be a **reason** for creation, necessarily requiring some external reference or alternative - in which case **known** creation cannot be **entire** creation, imperfecting any theories, principles, and laws thought to be universal?

And, eschatologically, why should the known universe be destroyed? A divine moral judgment [as conventional religions assume], or merely the same whim that engendered its creation? In that latter case it would follow that all efforts at virtue by universal inhabitants are futile, merely self-deceptive, purposeless abstinence from the fullest experience and expression of life.

Beyond the doctrinal confines of Judæo-Christianity these limitations evaporate. Non-linear time, as in the circular or cyclical cosmologies of antiquity, need neither origin nor originator, bur extend endlessly into the past as into the future. Existence similarly needs no excuse or cause, because it is just as primally-inherent as nonexistence. This may be a bit difficult for linear-trained minds to grasp, but it is helpful, if not essential to FF technology and application, as will be seen herein.

Throughout an eternal, omnipresent cosmos, its ordering, binding, and consistency principles - called [Egyptian] *neteru*, gods, or Pythagorean/Platonic Forms

- are also omnipresent and ageless, and of course need no rationale for their preservation of order.

(2) Natural Law

Natural Law is Eternal Law to the extent that human reason can detect consistent principles in the Objective Universe (OU). This process of detection and definition is called [physical] "science". As it is the extension of ineffable Eternal Law, it is presumed to be beyond justification, and also beyond violation.

Because of Natural Law's OUniversality it is problematical whether any part(s) of it could be broken by inquisitive or brash humans, if they wished to so attempt. Certainly any disruption such violation could cause would be chaotic in the extreme, perhaps to a disastrous degree.

One example of such "Natural Law blasphemy" might be the smashing of natural atomic structures in order to release the power therein, as was done at Los Alamos in 1945 at the culmination of the Manhattan Project. The result was the unleashing of a concentration of power never otherwise existing apart from stars such as Earth's Sun. Decades later the Earth is still endangered by the consequences of that experiment, as manifest in PhysWar's forest of thermonuclear weapons.

(3) Divine Law

Divine Law governs human behavior concerning Natural Law - prescribing its use and proscribing its abuse - as directly revealed of the mind of God through the media of Judæo-Christianity, e.g. its "Old Testament" prophets, Jesus Christ and his "New Testatment" spokesman, and the Jewish/Christian institutions making pronouncements on their behalf.

Similar non-Christian authority is also claimed by Judaism's other principal spin-off, Islam.

Such Divine Law, since it is deemed to emanate from the Godhead. is held to be absolutely mandatory and superior to the fourth and lowest category, Human Law. Examples are the *Holy Bible* of J/C and the *Koran* of Islam. It will be noted that extraordinary political power accrues to individuals and institutions with the right to interpret such Laws.

This is of especial important in MW campaigns in which supranational religious values - perceived Divine Law - plays a part, because it controls the beliefs and behavior of involved humans more than is possible with any of their Human Laws. MW operators must assume control of Divine Law dictates through MWB's PSYCONs, and re-"interpret" them as necessary. It hardly need be noted that this requires the utmost sensitivity and precision to establish the required "authenticity", and that this is an extremely irrational and emotional environment of MW operation.

(4) Human Law

As Aquinas impressed it, Human Law comprises codes and conventions which humans and their political institutions create for themselves, and which, to be good and virtuous, should reflect the dictates of Divine Law and the principles of Natural Law. In other words, humanity should not make laws just for their pleasure or convenience, but in obedience to and conformity with higher laws. When the United States' founding documents, or those of the other great revolutions, invoked "endowed" and "inalienable" rights, they were calling upon this higher-law authority.

PhysWars, and replacement MW campaigns, find themselves in disputes often phrased as disagreements over national and/or international law. Once again it is essential to be sensitive to the authority claimed by all such laws, whether "merely" human or Divine/Natural-authentic.

Politically-atheistic nations - such as the United States, Europe, Russia, and China - are termed thus not because they don't have some religious population, but because their governance ignores Eternal, Natural, and Divine Law in their crafting of Human Laws. In some countries, indeed, any overtly-religious influence in lawmaking is expressly forbidden, as in the United States' "church/state separation" doctrine. This fact is not infrequently made more palatable to superstitious citizenry by the use of elaborate but vacuous invocations, blessings, holidays, etc.

c. MW Supertheism

From the above elaboration it follows that, to be effective in his craft, the MWarrior must not only not allow himself to be enslaved to any of the 95% Laws, but indeed must actively take control of, determine, and disseminate & "interpret" them. He must intentionally and convincingly play, if not be God in the MW campaign. In this role, to be sure, he must never make the mistake of falling victim to his own PSYCON, or he will simply have replaced one counterproductive array of counterproductive superstitions with another.

d. Machiavelli's Admonition

Niccolò Machiavelli [discussed in further detail below] contended that since Divine Law is beyond the comprehension of human reason, it cannot and should not be asserted as justification for social systems. Politics, he argued, belongs wholly to the realm of reason, and should be evaluated on that basis alone. "For the manner in which men live is so different from the way in which they ought to live that he who leaves the common course for that which he ought to follow will find that it leads him to ruin rather than to safety." This focus on exclusively human-formulated, achievable practicality (the *áristos*) ultimately encourages man to attain dignity by taking complete responsibility for himself.

MW therefore frequently confronts situations which, in "Law"-terms, are a destabilized, confused mix of Divine and Human Law, which it must remedy not just by taking control of both in the context familiar to the afflicted populace, but also by undertaking the construction of an *áristos* or *kalokagathia* independent of both conditioned constraints. Ironically such solution may, to gain popular credence and acceptance, need to be cloaked in Divine- and/or Human-Law masquerade.

7. Sciences

a. Physical: Natural aw

When physical scientists identify a problem in their respective discipline, they address it against a standard of reality - "scientific law" - which they have carefully and laboriously developed over the entire course of human history. Thus a problem in mathematics is first articulated, then specified, then finally calculated and solved by and within accepted mathematical laws. It is simply a matter of "plugging the problem in" to those laws, then calculating its resolution accordingly.

b. However ...

There are of course cheats.

Sometimes when a new problem doesn't fit completely and comfortably into the "sacred reality" of the accepted standard, it is not permitted to offend that god, but is simply rephrased to force it to fit, like Cinderella's glass slipper being replaced with a larger one to satisfy the ambitions of her stocky stepsisters. [1]

In especially sacrilegious situations wherein a new problem not merely annoys, but explodes core assumptions of the accepted standard, it may be dealt with by simply ignoring it - as for instance the question of how a pre- "Big Bang" clump of universal matter/energy (*ylem*) came into being and who touched a match to it to initiate the "expanding universe". [2]

As long as these two rugs exist under which annoyances can be swept, the physical sciences can at least pretend to respectability.

c. Social: No Law ∴ No Science

With the social sciences it is a different matter. The conventional wisdom is that they are not indeed "real" sciences at all, because science requires a rigid, laboratory-repeatable standard of natural law. The social sciences, however, all involve the supposed wild card of "human discretion", which is generally assumed to be whimsical, hence unpredictable. So Political Science, History, Sociology, and Anthropology have all devolved into the mere recording and critical evaluation of past events.

---

[1] "Never let an inconvenient fact spoil a good theory." - Wolfram Hanrieder, Professor of Political Science, University of California, [jokingly] to the author as a graduate student ca. 1975.

[2] "[Tools for scientists include] a magnifying glass for the detection of imperfections, and a can of black spray paint to instantly cover up inconvenient imperfections." - Anton Szandor LaVey, High Priest of the Church of Satan, ca. 1970.

d. However ...

In the case of Political Science this reticence is arguably unjustified. Human thinking and behavior **can** be predicted at both the individual and the mass level.

As the author's companion book in this series, *MindWar*, explains and details, human actions result from individuals' perception of "reality", collected into "thought patterns" assembled in the subconsciousness: overwhelmingly the product of similarly-subconscious sensory input. As *MindWar* further proposes, shape those inputs through psychological control artifice (PSYCONs) and you shape the derived reality-patterns, consequently the boundaries and tendencies of behavior within them.[3]

In addition to the recognition and control of human behavioral mechanisms, a schematic is needed for the coherent identification, analysis, resolution, and consequent outcome of a social problem. Here too the *stats quo* is woefully inadequate, indeed chaotic.

Because it is taken for granted that human behavior is unpredictable, no attempt to address issues beyond the immediate alleviation of emotions is made. The only "extensions into the future" considered are those of presumed permanent force, such as national territorial borders and sovereignty. The result is little more than a succession of temporary "bandages", lasting only until a next one is necessary. Summarily: chaos held only temporarily at bay.

---

[3] Aquino, Michael A., *MindWar*. San Francisco: Barony of Rachane, 2013, 2016.

B. *Status Post*: FindFar

Having recognized that human behavior is both predictable and controllable, the next step is to develop a mechanism to accomplish both methodically, wisely, and constructively when applied to potential, incipient, or existing problem situations. Instead of endlessly and inadequately bandaging chaos, we shall eliminate it in favor of a coherent, ordered, and beneficial future: Plato's *kalokagathia*.[4]

Crucial to this adventure is that mere prediction - or social-scientific "forecasting" - is not enough; too often that assumes merely anticipating the probability of futures of alternative chaotic-bandaging. *Kalokagathia* demands that the entire process be ordered and controlled towards a predetermined outcome. The vehicle this book presents to effect this is characterized by "the finding of the far" in capabilities, capacities, and courses of action, thus:

As both an analytical and a practical tool, FindFar (hereinafter "FF") serves as the "reverse-engineering" component of MindWar ("MW"), through which the best possible practical outcome (*áristos*[5]) is traced back to the present by its progressively-necessary decisions and

---

[4] The ancient Greek term καλοκαγαθία. As developed by Plato in the *Gorgias*, *kalokagathia* identifies "moral virtue reflecting both the natural and the conventional": the key to both individual and community perfection.

[5] *Áristos* (from the ancient Greek αρίστος): The best for a given situation. - John Fowles, *The Áristos*, 1964.

actions. Thereby a MW campaign is "mapped" to its intended accomplishment.

C. FF Inspiration: Machiavelli

To the establishing of Political Science as a science, *FindFar* begins where *MindWar* concluded: with Niccolò Machiavelli (1469-1527), who is famed for, among other things, being the first political scientist [as opposed to philosopher or theorist], by seeking to describe human politics as it is, not as it ought to be.

Amidst the instability of Renaissance Italy, Machiavelli sought in his writings, most notably *The Prince*, to guide rulers of the various city-states towards the establishment and maintenance of functional and stable societies. In essence he sought an applied *kalokagathia* embodying the *áristos*, much the same as modern statesmen are challenged to do. A closer examination of *The Prince* reveals that it is no mere collection of antiquated aphorisms, but a very timely prescription for FF refinement.

1. *Fortuna*: Four-Dimensional Reality

Prior to Machiavelli political philosophers considered incidents and issues as static questions: Either they were abstract principles to be apprehended and approximated to the rational, or they were set-piece, unique situations to be solved as such. They were not a sequence, process, nor process. As such they were three-dimensional, occupying a momentary displacement in space.

To this model Machiavelli added the fourth dimension of **time**. For him, political problems were not static, but **dynamic**, indeed necessarily so. Indeed it was precisely this dynamism which made them destabilizing. Consequently they could only be solved through 4-

dimensional strategies, designed and adjusted to match and control the problems' dynamic.

Machiavelli saw the chaotic 4th dimension as a haphazard environment of happenstance and accident, which he summarized as *fortuna*. *Fortuna* underlay every political problem; therefore the initial task was to recognize and define it according to its constituent factors.

To be valid beyond a purely parochial - hence artificial and ultimately misleading - level, any description of *fortuna* must include proportionate consideration of the aforementioned global problems. These should not, however, be allowed to overwhelm the immediate, localized issue to the point of stymying MW efforts to alleviate it: once again the allegory of the starfish.

2. *Virtu*: Controlling the Dimensions

To overcome, compensate, and neutralize *fortuna*, Machiavelli advocated a proactive and relentless campaign of rationality, reason, and practicality which he called *virtu*. [Today we would call it a "MW campaign".] Significantly [and somewhat confusingly to modern ears], *virtu* did not include a "morality" aspect: it addressed problems strictly in terms of cause-and-effect, hence solutions similarly. Benign solutions might [and should] suffice for benign situations, but harsh ones might require equally-harsh corrections. It is from this blithe pragmatism that Machiavelli received an "evil" image, even to the darkly-comic extent of the Devil being given the additional appellation of "Old Nick".

Machiavelli never proposed that "ends justify means". The correct quote from *The Prince* #XVIII reads:

> Moreover, in the actions of all men, and most of all of Princes, where there is no tribunal to which we can appeal, we look to results. Wherefore if a Prince succeeds in

establishing and maintaining his authority, the means will always be judged honorable and be approved by every one. For the vulgar are always taken by appearances and by results, and the world is made up of the vulgar, the few only finding room when the many have no longer ground to stand on.

Virtu is the element of MW analysis in which identification of preexisting, "invisible" Eternal, Natural, and Divine Law takes place. Indeed they **determine** the existing presumption of *virtu*. It is precisely this standard, to the extent that it is responsible for the existing problem, which MW must supplant.

3. *Necessita*: Moderating Change

Having conceived *virtu* as an aggressive, active antidote to *fortuna*, Machiavelli cautioned that in containing the extremes of chaos, the solution wasn't applied so forcefully as to only displace one chaos with another. *Virtu* should be prudent and limited, just enough to neutralize existing hazards and/or prevent looming ones: a regimen of the minimal employment of power and force which he called *necessita* - literally "the necessary".

With regard to *necessita* Machiavelli was especially concerned with "economy of violence", emphasizing that it should be resorted to not just minimally but as briefly as possible, that it might be just as quickly forgotten by the populace. [Pleasantries, on the other hand, should be extended over time to maximize their appreciation.]

Once again the aforelisted global issues have a direct bearing upon *necessita*, because some of them are "ticking time-bombs" with varying impact upon the specific problem addressed in a MW campaign.

If, for example, the immediate concern is internal instability in Bangladesh, due consideration in any solution must include the **global-warming** prognosis that the entire country will be engulfed by rising **ocean** during the 21st century, incidentally aggravating the worldwide **refugee** problem with its displaced 150 million **population** looking for new places to live.

Disputes between India and Pakistan cannot be addressed in disregard of their both being **nuclear-weapons** nations, with any such resort by either of them triggering **environmental contamination**, **health**, and "domino" **PhysWars** elsewhere.

4. *Occasione*: Timing is Everything

A key corollary of Machiavelli's sensitivity to time was his insistence that, to have maximum effect, applications of *virtu* must be precisely aligned to opportune moments and trends: *occasione*. Implementing a strategy too early or too late could not only be ineffective but even aggravate or complicate the problem it was designed to solve.

The tacit assumption is "the sooner the better", and if there is extraordinary suffering involved, this stands to reason. Nevertheless artificial changes, such as involved-countries' administrations, scheduled international conferences, pending economic negotiations/aid, etc. may impair or expedite MW solutions, as may natural conditions such as seasonal weather patterns and projected industrial or agricultural phases.

The ideal *occasione* is one in which the MW solution appears the least intrusive and jarring to local expectations. The more such involvement is perceived as rescue and relief rather than invasion or domination, the better its chances for positive reception and ultimate success.

5. *Ordini*: To What End?

As a practical political scientist, Machiavelli was neither an idealist nor a perfectionist. Moreover he was not a metaphysician in quest of some transcendental nobility in the human soul. Drawing rather upon the Stoic principles of the Roman Empire, he sought his version of the *áristos*: a "best possible cooperative stability" that he called *ordini*, "good order". Indeed the establishment of *ordini* would engender its own climate of practical ethics: *civitas* (again after the ancient Roman precedent of individual and collective civic duty and responsibility).

The discerning Classical historian may well object that Machiavelli's adulation of Rome is rather too glib: Even as a republic Rome struggled with many inequities and inadequacies, and its eventual collapse into Imperial despotism came as almost a relief to centuries of factionalism, demagoguery, and endless PhysWar. Marcus Aurelius' elegant Stoicism can be seen as more wistful aphorism than actual practice. Marcus himself didn't acquire or retain his throne by being the "Mr. Nicc Guy" of his celebrated *Meditations*!

Machiavelli was similarly no slave to ideology, including his own or that of his Princely patrons. Whatever succeeded, whatever came right to the point, was his focus, with ideological models or labels being after-decoration. Quoth Miles Davis: "I'll play it first and tell you what it is later."

D. FF Analysis: Reflection

In formulating his application of solutions to *fortuna*, Machiavelli also examined the way in which existing situations and problems are identified and analyzed:

reflective [as contrasted to impulsive or emotional] **thinking**.

Authentic reflection requires active, continuing attention to factors relevant to practical solutions under consideration. Conclusions must draw upon both **observations** of the problem and accumulated **knowledge** concerning its past history and present profile. Additionally current observations must be considered in light of past experience to assess their consistency and reliability.

1. Logic

The culmination of reflection is **logical analysis**.

Logic is that branch of philosophy which attempts to determine when a given statement or group of statements permit some other statement to be verified.

As a strict academic discipline logic attempts to distinguish verifiable inferences from inconclusive ones. It is approached through a comparison of statements, drawing conclusions from both knowledge and observation according to one or more of three processes: **deduction**, **induction**, and **abduction**:

a. Deduction

Deduction draws firm conclusions from two or more facts whose combination inescapably leads to those conclusions.

Obvious care must be taken to ensure that the constituent facts are themselves valid, and that the applied conjunction is an appropriate, material one. All too often deductive conclusions are "set ups": the apparently-reasonable, even indisputable outcome from selectively-staged or -weighted "facts". In such cases deductive logic is merely a device to lend conclusions a veracity and inevitability which the raw data do not justify.

b. Induction

Induction seeks to draw probable conclusions from inconclusive information and/or sources of varying reliability. The result is thus a judgment-call by the evaluator.

Deduction is obviously preferable to induction, but both have their imperfections: deduction in the case of ill-chosen determinants, and induction in overreaching the basis or significance of the input information.

Even more in the case of induction there is a propensity for predetermining a desired conclusion by staging the "analysis".

c. Abduction

Abduction, the most precarious of the three, involves the critical comparison of two or more deductions and inductions on the basis of plausibility.

Abduction thus has two inherent weaknesses: reliance upon pre-flawed deduction or induction, and evaluation on the basis of plausibility, not truth *per se*. This second failing recalls what Plato warned against as the "democratization of truth", in which reality is established on the basis of popular sentiment rather than impersonal fact. The former is the province of demagoguery and what Plato disparaged as "sophism"; the latter characteristic of philosophers and dialectic reasoning.

2. Logical Fallacies

In addition to the hazards of logic stemming from either careless or weighted material from which to deduce, induce, or abduce, there are a number of fallacies which may appear, again either innocently or manipulatively, within a logical exercise itself. The MWarrior will need to be alert for them accordingly, including possibly within his own analytic efforts if he is inattentive to his own biases and assumptions.

Recall that the logician does not talk with reference to truth, ideals, or morality, but rather in terms of **verification** and **proof**. There are eleven specific invalidations that apply to these objectives:

a. Quoting Out-of-Context

Extremely common in contemporary news reporting and commentary, this technique extracts a passage, sentence, or larger statements or writings which by itself may seem to have one meaning when, contained within its complete utterance, may mean something quite different, even contradictory.

More subtly, and more proliferate in academia, policies and statements which may have served a desirable or necessary purpose in, say, the midst of World War II, can appear extrme, insensitive, unjust in later peacetime.

The "internment of enemy aliens" following Pearl Harbor is a classic example - as would be old practices of racial, religious, ethnic, or gender discrimination here and elsewhere.

This vulnerability highlights the importance of context itself as an analytical factor. An ideology or governmental structure which Americans may consider the "height of civilization" for themselves may be regarded as nothing of the sort in other countries or geographic areas. The blind advocacy of "democracy" sounds appealing on its face, but imposed on a culture with rampant illiteracy and a mood of mob-desperation throughout its "electorate" could presage disaster. It is vital for MW solutions to be contextually tailored to the people directly impacted, not to the preferences of distant do-gooders.

b. Sentimental Argument

Attempts to "prove" a statement by citing its popularity are invalid. While this should seem self-evident, it is both more prevalent and more insidious in practice, invoking as it does the consolation of "common sense".

At the time of this writing the United States is convulsed in argument over "illegal aliens" aka "undocumented immigrants". The very phraseology predetermines the tone of the debate, of course.

Both proponents and opponents appeal to sentiment: sympathy for the downtrodden simply seeking a better, safer life; vs. protection and preservation of the United States' somewhat nebulous image as a "Norman Rockwell" enclave perhaps realized only on Main Street in Disneyland. Authentic logic should eschew both emotions and focus rather on the economic and population-density changes accompanying open, closed, or varying-controlled national borders. Related, obviously, is the question of what if anything to do about accumulated past inattention to these questions: deportation, amnestic assimilation, or some hybrid of both. Either way sentiment, while tempting and compelling, can only hinder a logical resolution.

c. Authoritarian Argument

Attempting to prove a statement by citing a distinguished or important person or institution who endorses it is logically invalid.

This is a sort of stratified variation of the "democratization of truth" fallacy, attempted in a hierarchical or privileged environment.

In extreme situations it also refers to proclamations of "fact" by dictators, military commanders, "infallible" popes, and similar personages or institutions in a position of coercive authority. In George Orwell's *1984* "reality" is what the Party decrees it is, and any dissent whatever is "thoughtcrime".

Here it may be well to point out that it is just as much a logical fallacy to "disprove" something because it is embraced by authority or tradition: the unsupportable extreme of nihilism.

d. Ambiguity

Ambiguity refers to words, phrases, or statements which were intended to mean one thing but are represented as meaning something else, for the deliberate purpose of "proving" a position or proposition.

To be a "defender of life" is a rallying-call among opponents of abortion, while quite obviously the phrase in an of itself extends far beyond that application. Additionally, of course, "life" itself is ambiguous as to where it starts and stops, and of what it consists while in existence.

Many if not all of the "great questions" have an element of ambiguity in them, particularly if either their substance or their purpose is not generally or clearly understood. What, for instance, is a "human right"? Who has the power to grant and/or enforce it? Why should it apply to the human species exclusively and not to all other forms of natural life? Is it a mere convention, an agreed-upon human conceit within a limited audience? Or should it be limited to Aquinas' Human Law, reflective of and dependent upon Divine Law for its authority?

e. Interdependence

Two unproved statements cannot be used to prove one another.

Classical philosophers have enjoyed a field day playing with paradoxes and "vicious circles" of conceptual impossibility. "Roger Rabbit maintains that all rabbits are liars.": Are we to believe this statement?

Less entertainingly, nations routinely claim that they are forced into war by another's "threat", and that the "threat" is proved by that nation's armed retaliation. The "logic" of the war is thus established. No, it isn't: The initial perception of "threat" may have been innocently mistaken, or not-so-innocently fabricated, even to the extent of a "false flag" provocation-excuse.

Within FF evaluation there is a further dynamic dimension involved. A provocative or triggering incidence cannot be considered in time-discrete isolation. Its motives and origins must be traced back through time, which one quickly realizes is a beginningless history of venge and revenge.

Thus Nazi Germany is understandable only in the aftermath of the Versailles Treaty, whose harshness is explained by the perceived grievances of the victors in World War I, whose origins came from ... *ad infinitum*.

It is because of this principle that MW does not seek "justice [for the past]" in its solutions, but rather an *áristos* that is forward-oriented.

f. Significance

Some statements are accurate only when viewed together with other statements concerning the same subject.

One example was introduced above: the internment of ethnic Japanese in the United States during World War

II. By itself this would seem inhumane and racist. However there was an extremely harsh war underway with Japan, and not all Japanese residing in the United States were U.S. citizens. Even some who were had a strong affinity for Japan and quasi-religious loyalty to the person of the Emperor. Nor were Japan's wartime intentions towards the United States at all clear: The Pearl Harbor attack seemed to signal territorial aggression similar to that of Japan's incursion into Asia; no one could be certain. If the internment was later deemed to be excessive and unneeded, that is decidedly with the 20/20 vision of hindsight.

g. *Argumentum ad Ignorantium*

It is illogical to say that a given statement is true just because there is no evidence to disprove it.

Just because Bigfoot or a Yeti has not yet been captured, or a corpse discovered, does not prove that such creatures don't exist. Since their existence has thus not be disproven, it stands to reason that they do in fact exist.

Well, no. All that it establishes is that this question lacks sufficient data to be answered one way or the other at this point in time.

In the political situations addressed by MW, some may well prove to be unresolvable at this time because of key *lacunæ*: information which is essential but not yet available. This may necessitate active measures in on-location intelligence by MetaForce Branch, and/or additional research by ParaPolitics Branch. Either way a campaign should not be developed or implemented until the necessary gaps have been filled.

h. Composition and Division

What is true of the whole is not necessarily true of the parts, and *vice-versa*.

Czarist Russia gradually built up an empire of several vassal states, which after the communist revolution became the Soviet Union. Following the Allied victory in World War II, additional Soviet suzerainty prevailed throughout the Warsaw Pact - as, arguably, was also the reality with United States domination over the NATO alliance in the West.

The situation has further complicated following the collapse of Soviet communism and dissolution of the U.S.S.R., and corresponding Western efforts to re-justify NATO, even to the extent of projecting it far into south Asia such as Afghanistan.

Meanwhile efforts to make sense of new/old nations such as Ukraine are confusing to say the least. Some elements advocate more separation from Russia and even inclusion in NATO, while others prefer something closer to the old Soviet Union.

Great Britain is currently going through the many complexities of disengagement from the European Community, which is further complicated by one of its own components, Scotland, reconsidering whether to extricate itself from the United Kingdom in order to remain in the EC.

These are but two examples of time/space-layered problems whose solutions depend upon what scope of complication they are required to address.

i. *Ignoratio Elenchi*

This occurs, sometimes amusingly, when a person proclaims that he is going to prove something, then actually proves something irrelevant to the claim.

In 1492 Columbus set out from Spain to prove that if he sailed westward long enough, he would reach India. As it happened, what he reached was the Western, not the Eastern Hemisphere, though that didn't stop him from claiming success and clinching it by calling the local inhabitants "Indians".

j. *Non Sequitur*

Arguments which do not logically substantiate their contentions. This can be by simple imprecision in reasoning, or by intentional effort to sell a desired but unsubstantiated conclusion.

A well-known current example would be that humans are responsible for global warming because greenhouse gasses contribute to global warming and humans contribute to greenhouse gasses. Here the *non-sequitur* is that global warming is not caused exclusively or even primarily by greenhouse gasses, nor are greenhouse gasses exclusively or primarily caused by human beings. Such *non-sequiturs* are ignored by activists whose goal is to attack the fossil-fuel industry; prior to "global warming" they simply sought other alarmist rationales, such as natural resource devastation or accident contamination. [This is not a condemnation of environmental activism *per se*, but only an observation concerning its facile resort to emotional overstatement.]

k. *Argumentum ad Hominem*

Attempting to disprove something by attacking the author or proponent is logically invalid.

Consider this statement:

> When one says that God provokes the lightning, that's true in a sense; but what is certain is that God does not direct the thunderbolt, as the church claims. The church's

explanation of natural phenomena is an abuse, for the church has ulterior interests. True piety is the characteristic of the being who is aware of his weakness and ignorance. Whoever sees God only in an oak tree or a tabernacle, instead of seeing him everywhere, is not truly pious. He remains attached to appearances - and when the sky thunders and the lightning strikes, he trembles simply from fear of being struck as a punishment for the sin he's just committed.

From now on, one may consider that there is no gap between the organic and inorganic worlds. Recent experiments make it possible for one to wonder what distinguishes live bodies from inanimate matter. In the face of this discovery, the church will begin by rising in revolt; then it will continue to teach its "truths". One day, finally, under the battering ram of science, dogma will collapse. It is logical that it should be so, for the human spirit cannot remorselessly apply itself to raising the veil of mystery without people's one day drawing the conclusions.

The Ten Commandments are a code of living to which there's no refutation. These precepts correspond to irrefragable needs of the human soul; they're inspired by the best religious spirit, and the churches here support themselves on a solid foundation.[6]

Before glancing at the footnote to see who said this, consider whether or not it favorably impresses you, and if so whether it makes any difference who voiced this opinion.

This will serve to illustrate the degree of coloration which the source of a statement places upon it in the eyes of audiences who are conditioned to accept or reject anything from that source.

Pure logic evaluates statements regardless of source, on their content and merit alone.

---

[6] Hitler, Adolf, remarks to Lieutenant General von Rintelen on the evening of October 24, 1941. *Hitler's Table Talk 1941-1944*, Cameron & Stevens translation from Martin Bormann's transcripts.

3. The Lesson of Logic

Authentic reflective thinking is a far cry from the mere conjuring of vague opinions - upon which unfortunately most conventional "political analysis" is actually based. All too often we are [mis]treated to the spectacle of policies, positions, and actions whose only basis is the whim or prejudice of the decision-maker, with "supporting facts" being cherry-picked, taken out-of-context, or even brazenly invented to fit the stepsister's foot. Clearly such sloppiness, stupidity, and/or dishonesty is completely unacceptable in FF - and in MW generally.

This long list of cautions about "thinking errors" may appear painfully excessive to a readership, indeed an age of "civilization" comfortably accustomed to having opinions with either no or the most flimsy and self-serving justifications. This is scarcely a new problem; it was the point of the entire corpus of Plato's *Dialogues* to expose it in the Athens of his day, and forcefully argue for a rigorous, factual, and honest alternative to this prevalent, popular sophistry. Socrates' thanks for this embarrassing message was condemnation to death.

> Did he himself still comprehend this, this most introspective of all philosophers? Was this what he said to himself at the end, in the wisdom of his courage to die? Socrates wanted to die: It was not Athens, but he himself who chose the hemlock; he forced Athens to sentence him. "Socrates is no physician," he said softly to himself. "Here death alone is the physician. Socrates himself has merely been a long time sick."[7]

In subsequent millennia Socrates' hemlocktail changed first into burning alive at the stake, and in our own "Postmodern" *décadence* to more decorous if just as

---

[7] Friedrich Nietzsche, *Twilight of the Idols* (1889).

terminal media-blacklisting, academic tenure-denial, and similar "shoot the messengerisms".

Proposing and conducting MW campaigns would be ever so much more welcome among policy-makers, easier to conduct, and flattering to memorialize if MW were allowed to participate in this same farce of comfortable and convenient self-deception. It must always refuse this sirens' song.

E. FF Continuum

A **continuum** is a coherent whole characterized as a collection, sequence, or progression of values or elements varying by minute degrees.

Therefore the application of FF to a given problem situation generates a continuum embracing it from a present reflection to a future *áristos* reflection, connected through time by a reverse-engineered MW campaign. As long as due care is taken with each of the components, the entire continuum is not only surprisingly easy but inevitable and infallible, because the continuum is not only comprehensive but self-adjusting in its progression.

Before proceeding to its implementation, it is necessary to more closely examine its most crucial dimension: **time**.

Chapter 2: Time

The present is the ever-moving shadow that divides yesterday from tomorrow. In that lies hope.
                                    - Frank Lloyd Wright

[Upon hearing of Daylight Saving Time] Only the white man would believe that you could cut a piece from the top of a blanket, sew it to the bottom of that blanket, and have a longer blanket.
                    - Allowat Sakima, Chief of the Lenni-Lenape

A. The Fourth Dimension

Chapter #1 introduced reflections, each consisting of three dimensions in space, connected and individually elasticized by a fourth: **time** (or duration). It is the existence of this fourth dimension (4D) that changes political problems and their solutions from static to dynamic, making them truly intelligible only as continua. The MWarrior, the FF investigator, must accordingly indwell these continua if he is to correctly perceive and adjust reality.

And so what exactly is that mysterious, elusive 4D? It is with us constantly, inescapably, yet we cannot see, feel, touch, hear, or otherwise apprehend it through our natural senses. So this chapter proposes to expose this ghostly god: to transform it from controlling to controlled, and ultimately to illuminate the Valley of the Shadow of Death which is its domain.

B. Definition

1. *Ding Nicht An Sich*

Time itself does not exist at all. It is something which exists only apart from itself, in the eyes and intelligence of a distinct consciousness. It is the language by which that external consciousness detects, estimates, measures, and compares the changes of and between existential phenomena displacing the three dimensions of physical extension in space. In principle, if there were no such changes, time would, and could, not exist.

2. Kant

This interpretation of time was most famously articulated by the German philosopher Immanuel Kant (1724-1804), who in his *Critique of Pure Reason* (1781) contended that space (Dimensions 1-3) ant time (Dimension 4) are independent of, yet dependent upon one another to make them sensible concepts. Summarily:

- Different times are successive, not coexistent.

- Different spaces are coexistent, not successive.

In other words, time is necessarily a **measurement of elapse**, which can exist only as a sequence, a continuum.

As for spatial objects or defined areas [of emptiness], they necessarily displace a single "point in time", more precisely a "moment **without** time" in order to be absolute in themselves: Two 3Ds cannot displace the same locus simultaneously.

3D space, Kant argued, is **objective**, that is independent of external perception.

Time, on the other hand, is **subjective**: It exists only in the mind of an external perceptive consciousness (5D), as an arbitrary, convenient means of demarcating changes in 3Ds themselves, and/or compared to other 3Ds. That time has the illusion of objectivity is merely because of conventions among perceivers as to a common standard of such measurement, such as a "minute" or "hour" based upon the Earth's solar orbit.

3. Einstein

This simple and self-evident distinction of Kant's would be attacked by Albert Einstein in his confusingly-named "theory of relativity", in which he insisted against all sanity that time is not a subjective relationship but an objective constant, thus mandating rigidly-calculated absurdities such as an everywhere-fixed velocity of light: leading to such derivative preposterities as "curved space" and "black holes". Eventually Pavlovian science will extricate itself from this tar-baby, or so one can only hope.

4. *Noumenon*

Since time is an arbitrarily-assigned valuation, Kant continues, it is not empirical: It is not gained or learned from observation of natural phenomena. Rather it is *a priori*; it is assigned to objective phenomena, including, significantly, **before** and **after** they occur. Such concepts would not be possible in a genuinely-empirical environment.

5. Objective Universal Dynamic

The natural, or more precisely objective universe (OU) of matter and energy [including their balancing/ offsetting anti- counterparts] is, completely and continuously, changing. This change permeates the OU from the quark to the metagalactic, and the first question is why this should be so. Why shouldn't the OU be everywhere static, a motionless "manifestation of death"? Why is it everywhere "restless"?

Further, why is this "restlessness" itself an OU-law, functioning uniformly everywhere? Science-fiction authors and mathematically-enthralled physicists have played with time-violations of various whimsy: warps, distortions, worm- & black-holes, jumps, alternate OUs, and of course the ubiquitous time-travel [as a sort of 4D Möbius strip[8] or Klein bottle[9]]. As entertaining as these fictional shortcuts and band-aids may be, they remain nothing more than that, to the inevitable, inescapable frustration and fury of the Einstein-gullible. [The still-enshrined "theories of relativity" demystify to mere sillyscience puffery of the prosaic fact that perceivers of changing objects simultaneously change in and between themselves - according to the very same OU-laws.]

_____

[8] The Möbius strip is a non-orientable surface with only one side and only one boundary. It is easy to create by taking a ribbon of paper, twisting one end 180°, and attaching it to the other end. It would be interesting to hear Chief Allowat's comments concerning such topological impudence.

[9] The Klein bottle is a non-orientable surface; it is a 2D manifold against which a system for determining a normal vector cannot be consistently defined. Informally, it is a one-sided surface which, if traveled upon, could be followed back to the point of origin while flipping the traveler upside down. Offered the experience, Chief Allowat declines such an indignity.

C. History, or "Reality Control"

Before proceeding into the consideration of time as a means for comprehending the present and controlling the future, it will be useful to examine how it has been used and misused retrospectively:

> The Party said that Oceania had never been in alliance with Eurasia. He, Winston Smith, knew that Oceania had been in alliance with Eurasia as short a time as four years ago. But where did that knowledge exist? Only in his own consciousness, which in any case must soon be annihilated. And if all others accepted the lie which the Party imposed - if all records told the same tale - then the lie passed into history and became truth. "Who controls the past," ran the Party slogan, "controls the future; who controls the present controls the past." And yet the past, though of its nature alterable, never had been altered. Whatever was true now was true from everlasting to everlasting. It was quite simple. All that was needed was an unending series of victories over your own memory. "Reality control" they called it; in Newspeak "doublethink".[10]

"History" is something we can count on as a standard of morality, as hard evidence of truth, as bedrock amidst our whirling contemporary environment of uncertainties, right?

Wrong. Historical accounts are written by human beings with widely-varying backgrounds, perspectives, motives, and paychecks. Even given perfect, immediate access to all information about an event, no two people will describe it, or its significance, in the same way. And in historical research there is almost never access to all relevant information to begin with.

Daniel J. Boorstin is Librarian of Congress Emeritus, and is a distinguished scholar and Pulitzer Prize winner who has authored many superb historical analyses. In his

---

[10] Orwell, George, *1984*. New York: Signet Books, 1949, page #32.

Hidden History he proposes several laws that shape what we know as "history":[11]

(1) **The Law of the Survival of the Unread**
There is a natural and inevitable tendency toward the destruction and disappearance of documents most widely used; therefore there is an inverse relationship between the probability of a document surviving and its value as evidence of the daily life of the age from which it survives.

(2) **Survival of the Durable and That Which is neither Removed nor Displaced**
Tombs, burial objects, mummies, temples, churches, and pyramids tend to skew our view of the past. They give a prominence to religion in the relics of the past which it may not actually have had in the lives people lived.

(3) **Survival of the Collected and the Protected**
= What goes in government files. We emphasize political history and government in the life of the past partly because governments keep records while families and other informal groups seldom do.

---

[11] Boorstin, Daniel J., *Hidden History: Exploring Our Secret Past.* New York: Vintage Books, 1989.

(4) **Survival of Objects Which are not Used or Which Have a High Intrinsic Value**
It is not only in printed matter that rarity and scarcity induce survival. Treasured or hoarded artifacts frequently survive where commonly-used, more representative ones do not.

(5) **Survival of the Academically Classifiable and the Dignified**
Teachers teach the subjects in which they have been instructed.

(6) **Survival of Documents which Pertain to Controversies**
What often passes for the history of a practice, belief, or institution is more accurately the history of controversies about it.

(7) **Survival of the Self-Serving: The Psycho-Pathology of Diarists and Letter-Writers**
Historians are urged to seek records by participants in events, preferably those made at the time or soon thereafter. Such are often self-serving and egotistical at the expense of objectivity.

(8) **Survival of the Victorious Point of View: The Success Bias**
If an invention, trend, or point of view prevailed, it and its proponents are

assumed to be representative rather than failed or minority alternatives.

(9) **Survival of the Epiphenomenal**
People often write and read books because they cannot personally experience what is described. It is often uncertain whether a writer is recording or escaping an experience.

(10) **Knowledge Survives and will be accumulated over Time, but Ignorance Disappears**
The mind of the modern historian has access to the accumulated knowledge and experience of the ages since the period of the past he is trying to recapture, but for this reason he cannot see reality as the people of that time saw it.

What are the implications of this for the MWarrior? It means that:

- **All** of the historical sources you consult are incomplete, inaccurate, biased, and/or incompetent to some degree.

- You **yourself** are in the grip of tacit prejudices and presuppositions which you have never questioned or even acknowledged as anything **to** be questioned.

You can compensate for #• by going outside "blessed" history sources to others, including those of the "enemy" (then or now) in order to examine the events in question from as many perspectives as possible. You can compensate for #•• by consulting third parties - including the "enemy" (then or now) - for their assessments of the issue, which you can then evaluate along with your own towards that eventual, vital **objectivity.**

D. Patterns

1. OU-Reality Construction

MindWar introduced and emphasized the significance of "**pattern thinking**", by which the subconscious human mind constructs, maintains, and adjusts "models" or "benchmarks" of what is assumed to be Objective Universe (OU) -real [as opposed to Subjective Universe (SU) -imaginary].

It is the presence of such patterns, which more-or-less interlock into a "coherent whole", that enables humans to function in the OU, including between themselves.

Subconscious pattern-thinking utilizes approximately 95% of human thinking, relegating what humans regard as conscious, or "algorithmic", thinking to the remaining 5%.[12] Subconscious patterns, significantly, are not in themselves dynamic; they are "3D snapshots" of reality compositions, not 4D "storylines" [through time].

2. In/Sanity

a. *Exposé*

Individuals without such thought-patterns, or with ones inconsistent with socially common/endorsed ones,

---

[12] Cf. Leonard Mlodinow, Ph.D., *Subliminal: How Your Unconscious Mind Rules Your Behavior* (New York: Pantheon, 2012).

or discretely-changing ones, are classified [by society-anointed "reality authorizers" such as psychiatrists and conventionally-sanctioned-religious clergy] as "insane".

"Sanity" is established by an individual's agreement with the generally-approved pattern of OU-reality; inability or refusal to endorse this established-consensus is deemed to be a "breakaway" from it, schizophrenia.

In fact, apart from physical brain injury or illness, there are many reasons why an individual's thought-patterns may not mirror socially-proclaimed ones. Actually no two individuals share precisely or even closely the same sensory perceptions, so "sanity" is more accurately a trained, conditioned individual conformity to social expectations. It cannot be called true connection with the OU; rather what humans consider "OU-reality" is more properly described as an officially-agreed-upon common SU-image of the OU.

b. The Ministry of Love

In *1984* George Orwell's society-spokesman O'Brien admonished the recalcitrant Winston Smith:

> You are here in the Ministry of Love because you have failed to control your memory. You have failed in humility, in self-discipline. You would not make the act of submission which is the price of sanity. You preferred to be a lunatic, a minority of one.
> Only the disciplined mind can see reality.
> You believe that reality is something objective, external, existing in its own right. You also believe that the nature of reality is self-evident. When you delude yourself into thinking that you see something, you assume that everyone else sees the same thing as yourself.
> But I tell you that reality is **not** external. Reality exists in the human mind and nowhere else. Not in the individual mind, which can make mistakes and in any case soon perishes, but in the mind of the Party which is collective and immortal.

> Whatever the Party holds to be truth **is** truth. It is impossible to see reality except by looking through the eyes of the Party.
>
> That is the fact that you have got to relearn. It needs an act of self-destruction, an effort of the will. You must humble yourself before you can become sane.[13]

As will be evident from the preceding discussion, O'Brien's elucidation was by **no** means just dramatic-fictional exaggeration, appropriate to dismiss right after its tickle.

The only difference between Orwell's world and ours is that the environment of Oceania and its Party is much simpler and more overt in its demands and punishments. In contemporary actual society there is still the same implicit expectation that "sane" people passively and automatically embrace the proclaimed, established, and enforced "Collective Subjective Universe" (CSU). Unlike Orwell's capital-punishment "Thoughtcrime" intolerance, consequences range from mere indulgence as an "eccentric" to ostracism or confinement as "insane". Specific consequences reflect the perceived severity of CSU-challenge by the individual in question.

c. "00Ψ": License to Instill

Political CSUs differ from culture to culture, nation to nation. Where ordinary socialization appears inadequate, they are enforced by conventional, crude thought-control such as propaganda.

The identification of propaganda and similar thought-control devices, from the mildest commercial advertising to unendurable physical/mental stress (*1984*'s "Room 101") is the initiatory education of governmental Psychological Operations (PSYOP)

---

[13] *1984, op. cit.*, pages #205-6.

professionals. An unspoken but very real element of such training is that the officer must ultimately not only become aware of his and others' societal "matrix" [as in the celebrated science-fiction film of that name], but step outside of all such CSUs [thus "taking the red pill"] in order to manipulate them. The risk is that, once entrusted with such "oo-license", he will be unreliably free from his own, not just others' matrix. Conventional PSYOP officers, while indeed suspect and mistrusted in this regard, are paradoxically not eliminated outright because they are also considered only peripherally competent in their craft.

MindWar as revealed and detailed in this series of books - *MindWar*, *MindStar*, and now *FindFar* - is very obviously a complete game-changer. The initiated MWarrior, like Caine receiving the Shaolin brands of the dragon & tiger in *Kung Fu*, now posses thought-control skill of a literally divine potency. Were profane society to realize this, his life would be instantly forfeit. Fortunately the true significance of MW is far beyond the conceptualization of the "unbranded", as well it should and must remain: An entire world rampant with such knowledge would be not an opportunity for enlightened *áristos* or *kalokagathia*, but an orgiastic apocalypse of evil: the *id*-monster of *Forbidden Planet* triumphant.

E. Memory

Memory is the "past" 4D function of human thought-architecture, and exists exclusively in the conscious 5% of algorithmic thinking. [Subconscious patterns may contain elements of past experiences, of course, but themselves have no 4D-depth.]

Conventional, traditional efforts to communicate with and convince others in a sociopolitical environment have been overwhelmingly limited to argumentative appeals and exhortations to this conscious 5%, which is precisely why, as *MindWar* demonstrates, they never work. Throughout human history, from antiquity to the beleaguered 21st-century, only a few fragments of intended information reach their audiences, and even these are mostly misunderstood and quickly forgotten. Why? Again the answer is found in thought-architecture, specifically with regard to humans' processing of conscious, "episodic" memory.

1. Attention

You've got only six minutes to make your point. [14]

And that's only if and after you've gotten your audience's attention in the first place - which, in the Age of the Internet - is often limited to the time/space of one or two sentences. [15]

So insists Ron Hoff, one of the advertising industry's most effective representatives. [16]

So what's magic about "six minutes"? That, argues Hoff, is the effective attention-limit of an audience in any presentation setting such as a classroom, auditorium, or

---

[14] Hoff, Ron, *Say It in Six: How to Say Exactly What You Mean in 6 Minutes or Less.* Kansas City, MO: Andrews McMeel Publishing, 1996.

[15] There is no more dramatic illustration of this than the worldwide, spectacular success of "Twitter", a medium of Internet sound-bites. In 2016 the United States, traditionally the preserve of long-winded speechifying, arguably elected its next President, Donald Trump, on the effectiveness of his "tweets" - which, in his administration, will presumably obsolesce Franklin Roosevelt's famous, but intolerably slow "fireside chats".

[16] In addition to conducting hundreds of nationwide presentations, Hoff has been a frequent contributor on communication effectiveness to media such as the *New York Times*, the *Wall Street Journal*, and the *Chicago Tribune*.

conference room. Beyond that listeners' thoughts begin to wander and retention of further points evaporates.

Therefore, he advises, condense the most important points - the ones you **really** want the audience to "take away" with them - into those precious first-six. If you feel the need for elaboration, provide a handout, write a paper, publish a book.

Unfortunately most people don't know how to write effectively either, which cripples if not nullifies any such platform. As with speaking, a document has only a brief shot at a reader's attention, so if you want him to continue past the dust-jacket teaser, you'd better learn the ropes and lasso him forthwith.

Effective writing, like effective speaking, has suffered a lingering starvation in the American educational desert. What was once drilled into high school students is now a rarity even at the university level. Fortunately the art survives in a few epistolary enclaves, and also in books such as the life-preserver I habitually toss to the frantically-floundering: *How to Write* by Herbert & Jill Meyer. [17] Like *SIi6*, *HtW* is a very slim book; both of them exemplify their own advice and do not waste either their pages or your eyes. If you want to maximize your effectiveness with **this** book, gobble both of those and keep each one on your bookshelf alongside it. Do it **now**.

2. Retention

Attention is only half the battle; the other half is ensuring that your recipients, whether audience or readership, not only remembers your message but does so accurately.

---

[17] Meyer, Herbert E. & Jill M., *How to Write: Communicating Ideas and Information*. New York: Barnes & Noble, 1994.

While subconscious thought-patterns tend to be rigid and permanent [as for example the significance of red/yellow/green traffic lights], conscious memory is comparatively brief and unreliable, even when sincere, serious concentration is attempted.

This frustratingly fickle conscious memory is known as **episodic** memory, since it is characterized by the "storyline" of 4D consciousness rather than the "snapshot" of 3D subconsciousness.

Ominously - especially in the context of political complexities and conflicts - this unreliability is not accompanied by a corresponding individual attitude of uncertainty. To the contrary, humans tend to cling to emotionally-cherished beliefs regardless of how objectively unsupportable they may be, until/unless irrefutable disproofs or contradictions are presented. Even then there is a tendency to avoid unpalatable refutations: to "not see" them or just change the subject. [18]

Just how pervasive is this episodic unreliability? In one study cited by the RAND Corporation:

> Weinshall had 34 executives in an industrial organization record their daily interactions for a two-week period. He found that 75% of the reported interactions registered in the mind of one party only. Of the 25% of communications which were mutually remembered a few hours after their occurrence, 53% were not understood by the recipient in the spirit intended by the transmitter. Thus of the total interactions reported, only 12% "got through". [19]

---

[18] In his searing satire *1984* George Orwell portrayed a then-fantastic, now all-too-extant political culture in which politically-incorrect opinions are neutralized through "doublethink", or which in extreme cases condemn the luckless "thought-criminal" to extermination and obliteration as an "unperson".

[19] Archibald, K.A., *Three Views of the Expert's Role in Policy-Making*. Santa Monica: RAND Corporation, 1970.

The key to retention is a corollary to the principles of *SIi6* and *HtW*: clear, undiluted, and well-substantiated "take-away" points.

3. Identity

Memory is also a key element of **identity**, the conscious awareness of unique selfhood. One of the traditional distinctions of humankind from other animals has been that non-humans live in a "perpetual present" of stimulus/response-only, and thus are not conscious entities. They experience 3D pattern-recognition, but not 4D "episodic" memory.[20] A cruelly-convenient extrapolation of this excuses reducing them to mere commodities which may be exploited, mistreated, and killed without conscience. Such a rationale is contemptuously callous on its face, amounting to nothing more than a judgment on the basis of non-verbalization rather than authentic non-feeling. It is yet another example of humans' propensity to refuse to confront shameful or frustrating inconveniences.

Just as identity of self is validated by 4D continuity, so are external phenomena. Cultures, nations, ethnic groups, and memori-als such as symbols and structures secure and sustain 4D (historical) significance to the extent they not only persist in their presence but are acknowledged by others. A revolution such as that of the United States is validated not just by its own assertion [as in military victory, the Constitution, etc.] but by its recognition in the international community. History abounds with examples of both successes and failures in this regard; at this writing the Islamic State conspicuously struggles to shed the dismissives of "self-

---

[20] Cf. Victoria L. Templer & Robert R. Hampton, "Episodic Memory in Nonhuman Animals", *Currnt Biology*, September 29, 2013:
   https://www.ncbi.nlm.nih.gov/pmc/articles/PMC3799964/

proclaimed" and "so-called". Conquerors regularly deny the "full-humanity" of the conquered, thus permitting their enslavement, expropriation, or extermination. In the most extreme and horrific instances, Orwell's *1984* prescription of "reality control" attempts to erase even the previous existence of a vanquished victim.[21] As dramatized by H.P. Lovecraft in his account of a New England eccentric murdered by his intolerant neighbors:

> From that time on the obliteration of Curwen's memory became increasingly rigid, extending at last by common consent even to the town records and files of the *Gazette*. It can be compared in spirit only to the hush that lay on Oscar Wilde's name for a decade after his disgrace, and in extent only to the fate of that sinful King of Runazar in Lord Dunsany's tale, whom the Gods decided must not only cease to be, but must cease ever to have been.[22]

F. Anticipation

The forward-looking counterpart to memory manifests in two general modes: passive and active.

1. Forecasting

Passively predicting or estimating the future course of events is called **forecasting**. FF begins with forecasting to establish a point of reference for the course of events absent active measures such as a MW campaign. Forecasting is discussed in detail in Chapter #3.

---

[21] Cf. #C above.

[22] Lovecraft, H.P., *The Case of Charles Dexter Ward*, 1927.

2. Foreshaping

Actively conceiving and controlling the future may take many forms, from modest adjustment of existing influences to ambitious social or even planetary engineering. When a MW campaign employs FF actively, to conceive, evaluate, and implement an *áristos*, it is called **foreshaping**. This concept is explained and expanded in Chapter #4.

G. Models

Time has also been interpreted as one of several models or frameworks by which humans measure their experience and understanding of the 4D. Interestingly these are not mutually-exclusive, and indeed can be applied cooperatively.

1. Circular

Probably the most ancient model of time is that it, as an indicator of natural change, moves in a continuous circle, the most obvious example of which being the rotating/repeating Sun every day and Moon every month, and beyond these the entire "stellar canopy" of the Zodiac.

Today, when one is engulfed in a linear-time environment, it requires an extraordinary effort of vacation to imagine the experience of conscious life within "circular nature". Very possibly mankind's first sense of alienation from nature, of being a "thing apart", was the realization that living beings did not participate in this endless, immortal circularity. Rather they were cursed, so it must have seemed, with linear finiteness: a unidirectional, inescapable trudge to death and obliteration. Worship of nature, of its gods or God, was nothing less than an appeal for a presumed re-inclusion in "lost" divine circularity: the Garden of Eden in which everything rotated but nothing changed.

In all religious, mythical, and fictional depictions of paradise, Heaven, or otherwise realms of the gods/God, the keystone characteristic is deathlessness by assimilation into unchanging circularity: consciousness verified by individual movement remains, but safely within eternal repetition.

To this day conventional religions promote this wistful hope, though in an OU everywhere awash in entropy, it is a concept ever more elusive for even itss proponents to visualize.

2. Cyclical

Again early in mankind's efforts to understand natural law, it was noticed that some events do not appear to exactly and endlessly repeat themselves, but do occur and recur at regular intervals, characterizing cycles. At their simplest, such cycles were identified in natural environments such as weather, rivers, and ocean currents and tides. Within the immediate human experience, and crucial to its continuation, were female fertility cycles.

Throughout recorded history the study of cycles has become ever more elaborate, extending even to the world of economics, as in the behavior of securities markets and the famous Kondratieff Cycle of strength and weakness.

In the realm of politics and conflict, alternations between PhysWar and peace, cooperation and isolation, relaxation and tension recurrently supersede one another, but it is questionable whether such movement between extremes is authentically cyclical, or more haphazardly just the irregular interplay of circumstances, strength, and weakness, both material and psychological.

3. Linear

A linear approach to time began most famously with Hebrew mythology, which postulated a fixed "Genesis" setting time in unidirectional motion, as well as a final end when all of the Hebraic god's interests are sated and human-inflicted tasks are completed. Such a fulfilling or catastrophic universal terminus is theologically termed "eschatology", and variations of it can be found in Christianity, Hinduism, Buddhism, and Islam. Curiously such "fixed. forced-march" pageants refuse to address the obvious *lacunæ* of what happened before the beginning or happens after the end.

Eschatology is most useful as a religious doctrine to compel human docility: Awaiting the obedient are personal posthumous rewards, while the disobedient face unimaginable punishment. So such doctrines have both an individual and a collective control-propaganda usefulness.

When Judæo-Christian mythology was discarded at the time of the European Enlightenment[23], the habit of linear history persisted, with Georg Hegel substituting an incorporeal, impersonal "God as history" for the celestial anthropomorph. Now the flow of events - the **dialectic** - was seen to be "the mind of this god seeking to fully understand itself through progressive ideas (**thesis**), their refutations (**antithesis**) and a resolving **synthesis** (which would thus become the successor thesis).

This comforting logical progression was disdained by Friedrich Nietzsche, who asserted history to be a chaos of "blindness, madness, and injustice". Post-Enlightenment

---

[23] The Enlightenment was a late-17th & 18th-century European philosophical, artistic, and scientific movement which, politically, proposed to replace secular monarchies with competing concepts of purely-human "social contracts" forcibly established, cooperatively negotiated, or spontaneously arising from public sentiment.

humans could not seek justification by a divinely-ordered history, even Hegelian-abstract, but most grapple with unfolding events on a completely-discrete, case-by-case basis.

Nietzsche notwithstanding, modern society still yearns for, and to a greater or lesser extent believes in events "reflecting God's will", as well as human PhysWar "blessed [or at least excused] by God", hence the proclamations, endorsements, absolutions, and other antics from international church executives down to military chaplains.

4. Relational

As this chapter establishes, actual time is nothing more than a standardized measurement of change within, without, and between 3D "events": objects or energies. There is in this standard no divine logic or law other than its consistency and uniformity throughout the Objective Universe (OU). Thus time is a tool applicable only to Natural Law.

Nor is time any semblance of an eschatological boundary, since it can be applied endlessly and limitlessly into the present, past, and future of Natural-Law events. For time to cease utility, the entire OU would have to unexist.

What this establishes within the context of MW and FF, is that considerations of 4D are **measurement tools only**, with no divine or other moral aspects whatever.

That said, the discerning MWarrior will be well-aware that conventional human PhysWar antagonists often enslave themselves to "divine purposes, expectations, or commands", thereby motivating their populations and armies as well as themselves. This enthrallment generates a MW PSYCON (Religion #13) vulnerability, which can thus be exploited as a powerful control device.

H. Time=God(s)

The culmination of Chapter #2 may come as a surprise, even a shock to readers. Reflect[24] upon it, however, and it will fall quite calmly and unremarkably into place:

Systematically, incre-mentally this chapter has led to the disarmingly-simple identification, indeed *exposé* of **4D as the actuality behind all concepts and images of an OU God/the gods**. In short, G/g equate to the totality of manifestations of change in the OU, within/without/between 3D matter/energy events. There is no possible conceptual manifestation otherwise.

The purpose of this statement is not to gratuitously shock reader composure with a dramatic theological *coup*. Understanding the actual mechanism of G/g does not in the least prevent or even discourage anyone's belief in G/g of choice, including endorsement of morality associated with that choice.

What **is** important here is that the MWarrior not be ignorant of that functional mechanism, so that its effects upon both self and others can be identified and if necessary adjusted through appropriate combinations of the MW PSYCONs.

Hence the task of the MWarrior is correspondingly simple: **Control time and you control G/g.**

More precisely, since the MWarrior conditions and adjusts humans in political situations, conflicts, and crises, control their **perception** of G/g through control of their perception of time/change in the OU.

---

[24] In the methodical, analytical discipline set forth in Chapter #1:D.

There is no need to assume or exercise an ostensibly religious role of any sort. Because of the actual identity of G/g as time, just adjust the humans' perception of time as necessary and they themselves will transform it into whichever of whatever G/g they worship and obey: theologic or symbolic.

Harking back to Chapter #1, this is indeed a modern Machiavellian prescription. Accordingly there is in this technique no moral aspect or agenda; its object is simply and directly the reduction, if not elimination of PhysWar mindless, unending, and excruciating mayhem in favor of "divinely mandated" relaxation and cooperation.

The following chapters, therefore, explore how 4D can be accurately identified and analyzed, and then how intelligent and constructive adjustments can be effected.

I. xD: Perspective

Establishing that any or all OU phenomena require and are identifiable in a complex of four OU dimensions necessitates that the perceiver be **external to and distinct from all of those dimensions**, else he would not be able to distinguish and differentiate each and all of them.

This is the essence of the individual awareness of self inherent in intelligent humanity. It exists, but neither in a 1-3D OU spacial displacement nor as a slave to OU time/ duration measurements (4D). It is in actuality OU-dimensionless and therefore OU-limitless. It exists only in and of itself, and has been clumsily identified in conventional cultures as the individual "soul". It may be apprehended and examined in precise detail in the second book of this trilogy, *MindStar*.[25]

---

[25] Aquino, Michael A., *MindStar*. San Francisco: Barony of Rachane, 2016.

While at first realization this OU-externality of individual consciousness may come as a shock to readers previously assuming themselves to be merely beings of and within the OU, once again the methodical exercise of reflective thinking will substantiate and indeed necessitate the OU-alienation which true and complete perspective requires.

When not dulled by habitual relaxation into passive physical-sensory stimulus/response metabolism, humans are therefore **pre**-universal entities in and of themselves: in reality and accuracy "gods".

This is not some mystical or theological conceit. It is prescient recognition of what enables the human mind to completely perceive and analyze OU phenomena, as MW requires.

Indeed once the MWarrior acknowledges his god-existence, it becomes a non-concern; what **is** important is the capacity for accurate perception and precise change that this essence imparts.

J. 5D: Creation

Once the existence and implications of xD are recognized, there is a further realization, once again as simple and inevitable as the xD god's passive powers: their active counterpart.

Just as each fully-sentient human has the ability to apprehend and understand the entire OU, so it follows that he can turn these same mental functions to **spontaneous creativity**: imagining and realizing new universes. Such are unique to each xD individual, hence are distinguishes as **Subjective Universes** (SU).

Unlike the single [known] OU, SUs are a prerogative of xD beings, not an establishment of law to which they are enthralled as caretakers and preservers. Thus an individual xD may create one, several, or no SUs, of equally-arbitrary 4D laws. The impact of such laws can range from the incidental to the maniacal, and from a stability similar to that of the OU to infinite flexibility. As Rod Serling so presciently summarized - and correctly "dimensionalized" it:

> There is a fifth dimension beyond that which is known to man. It is a dimension as vast as space and as timeless as infinity. It is the middle ground between light and shadow, between science and superstition, and it lies between the pit of man's fears and the summit of his knowledge. This is the dimension of imagination. It is an area which we call the Twilight Zone.[26]

K. FF Implications

Lest the reader be unnerved by this Indiana Jones jettison into strange dimensions and multiple universes, the point of this chapter is just to render coherent what is actually involved in the detection and evaluation of sociopolitical incidents and episodes.

This in turn clarifies what adjustments are possible and by what means they may be effected.

Finally the creative, generative capacity of the mind enables consideration of such adjustments to range beyond mere rearrangement of the known into actualization and augmentation from the unknown.

The next two chapters explore first the passive perceptive and analytical process (*fortuna*), then the active measures by which corrective change is introduced (*virtu/occasione*).

---

[26] Serling, Rod, original narrative introduction for *The Twilight Zone*, 1959.

Chapter 3: 3D Forecasting

Indiana Jones: [stares at Sallah] You said their headpiece only had markings on one side. Are you **absolutely sure**? [Sallah nods] Belloq's staff is too long -
[Together]: **They're digging in the wrong place!**
- Raiders of the Lost Ark, 1981

Professor Aronnax [anguished]: Yours was a dream of the future come true. I beg you to reconsider!
Captain Nemo [dying whisper]: A power greater than mine makes that impossible. But there is hope for the future. When the world is ready for a new and better life, all this will someday come to pass, in God's good time.
- 20,000 Leagues Under the Sea, 1954

A. Stasis Representation

Conventional analyses of current political problems fail to point the way to solutions for the reason expounded in the previous two chapters: They are static, 3D pictures of situations.

When tasked to be more elaborate, they expand again within the rigidity of a more detailed 3D picture. The result may be a proportionately clearer picture of the present state of affairs, but rarely a 4D exploration of past dynamics leading to it, and almost never a 4D dynamic beyond the present. Why should this be so?

1. Neglected Dentistry

If an international political situation has grown to the size of a current crisis, it obviously existed as a lesser disturbance in the past, whether for a short period or a longer duration. Either way, like a sore tooth, it was not prevented by attentive brushing and flossing, nor solved with a relatively minor filling once it became a cavity. Only now, when the pain has become intolerable and the sole remaining recourse is extraction or a root canal, is it being confronted.

Neither career diplomats nor intelligence agencies focus on "prevention". Their time, attention, and budgets are consumed by irons actually in the fire, nor do they wish to gain reputations as bearers-of-bad-news. So they remain reactive rather than proactive.

It is now well-known that both London and Washington had decoded the Japanese Pearl Harbor attack orders, but deliberately withheld notification of the military commanders in Hawaii so that a "minor raid" could be sensationalized to dislodge American isolationist sentiment. For its part Tokyo envisioned Pearl Harbor as something of a "bloody nose" to buy time and deter American intrusion into the western Pacific.

These naïve miscalculations went horribly wrong for both the United States and Japan. Admiral Yamamoto's bombers caught almost the entire Pacific Fleet at anchor, virtually annihilating it. To make matters worse, bungled Japanese embassy coordination in Washington delayed delivery of formal war declaration until after the raid, shaming it irretrievably as an unconscionable sneak-attack.

The catastrophic overconsequences stunned both nations. Roosevelt and Churchill got America's entry into the European war, but at the terrible price of four years' horrific slaughter in the Pacific, culminating in the nightmare of Hiroshima and Nagasaki. As for the Japanese, they were appalled by their success. "I fear all we have done," said Yamamoto upon learning of the devastation of the raid, "is to awaken a sleeping giant and fill him with a terrible resolve."

Through the lens of FF & MW, however, the **real** tragedy was failure of attention to the consequences of American commercial constraints on the Japanese economy over a much more extended prelude. Japan's perception was that this signaled an agenda of escalating hostility, quite possibly presaging eventual naval confrontation. MW monitoring and campaign initiation would have recognized both countries' perspectives and derivative motives, and neutralized them well in advance of their explosion into PhysWar apocalypse.

2. Doublethink

Also characteristic of more than a few nascent crises is a history of observer/analyst controversy over whether the subjects were initially or recently serious problems at all.

Government functionaries and bureaucrats, mindful of their careers, are understandably anxious not to gain reputations as incompetents or even "bearers of bad news"; too often the fire alarm is blamed for the fire.

It is always thought safer to reassure senior officials that their existing policies are wise and adequate. If and when they collapse, the usual recource is to foist the blame on "unforeseen factors" which no one could anticipate.

Even when an issue takes center-stage, disagreement often persists as to how significant it really is, whether it is a good or bad development; or even alternately both at once: Orwell's "doublethink".[27]

Is, for instance, the very existence of the United States of America historical legitimacy in which its citizenry have every right to take pride? Or is it land stolen from its original inhabitants, the American Indians, who were not only systematically dispossessed of their homeland but very nearly exterminated in the process?

If the latter, does the fact that this was an experience of previous generations excuse its results today?

Doublethink sympathizes with the Indians and weeps for their tragedy - but simultaneously dismisses any notion of returning their lands to them as inconceivable.

3. Thoughtcrime

Also as mentioned in Chapter #2, certain dilemmæ whose evident solutions touch or further fray "politically incorrect" nerves are both frequently and routinely dealt with by refusing to confront them at all, or by recontextualizing them into a admissible scenario.

At this writing persons entering the United States without government permission are styled either "illegal aliens" or "undocumented immigrants" depending upon the speaker's point of view. Persons denying women's right to control the functions of their own bodies style themselves "pro-life", while to the threatened women they are "anti-choice".

And of course nations as a whole prescribe certain terms while proscribing others. Whether you are a

---

[27] In the "negative utopia" of *1984*, words could have not only a variety of meanings, but even simultaneously inconsistent and contradictory ones, depending upon the motives and needs of a conversation. This convention goes beyond hypocrisy or duplicity to voluntary, automatic elasticity in the underlying thought itself.

"freedom fighter" or a "terrorist" is a decision reserved to your friendly neighborhood Thought Police. [28]

At the end of World War II the Allies felt sympathetic to [and tacitly guilty for their previous ignoring of] European Jews' suffering during the War, so the United Nations decided to give them a new, sovereign nation of their own.

Despite the fact that it was in Europe that the Jews had suffered, there was no question of any European nation, even the vanquished Germany and Italy [or the United States or Soviet Union], giving up any of their own territory for this magnanimous purpose.

Instead it was decided to give the Jews a completely-uninvolved third-party's land: that of Palestine.

The Palestinians themselves were not consulted in this decision. They were simply dispossessed by force - killed if necessary, and continue being progressively so to this day. Yet the justice of the original theft is not to be questioned: flouting of this taboo is agreed by the established international community to be thoughtcrime.

4. Tenacity

In a PhysWar analysis a crisis-potential problem such as that of Israel/Palestine is normally represented as a "current [3D] snapshot", with no attention or consideration paid to the 4D dynamic that engendered and aggravated it previously.

Correspondingly PhysWar-genre politicians are accustomed to looking for an equally-3D "solution of the

---

[28] In *1984* the most feared institution of domestic vigilance and surveillance is the Thought Police, which as its name implies is not concerned with overt acts, but rather with individuals' perceptions and opinions inconsistent with Party prescription and expectation. "Thoughtcrime is the crime that contains all others in itself."

moment" rather than a forward-evolving 4D dynamic as in a MW campaign.

An example of this is the 1962 Cuban Missile Crisis, wherein the United States suddenly discovered the Soviet Union to be moving nuclear-warhead intermediate-range ballistic missiles (IRBMs) into Cuba, capable of reaching almost the entire U.S.A. within 5-10 minutes.

This obviously, and drastically, reduced the United States' retaliatory response time from the previous ICBM window of 30 minutes, and was thus deemed unacceptable by the Kennedy Administration.

An immediate quarantine was announced, to be followed by an American air strike on and invasion of Cuba. The Soviet Union refused to remove the missiles, and a nuclear World War III appeared imminent.

At the last minute 4D review noted the previous presence of American Jupiter IRBMs in Turkey. Instead of the assumed mutual 30-minute launch warning, the U.S.S.R. had been living with, but evidently not comfortably, a 5-minute American launch warning. In their view comparable Soviet IRBMs in Cuba simply restored rather than destabilized deterrence balance.

The crisis was accordingly ended when both nations agreed to remove their IRBMs, restoring a mutual 30-minute window. [29]

The absence of a continuing 4D dynamic in the crisis' aftermath created a post-3D-solution vacuum of inattention, with dire consequences - once again quite susceptible to FF anticipation and neutralization. When word of the secret Jupiter deal eventually got out,

---

[29] Or so it was represented. In actuality both the U.S. and the U.S.S.R. had fleets of submarines armed with nuclear missiles capable of positioning themselves for launch much closer to the target(s) than either Turkey or Cuba. But being PhysWar-unsolvable, this even greater danger was tacitly ignored. In MW it would not have been, and would also have been neutralized.

President Kennedy was excoriated as being "soft on communism" - an albatross around his neck that contributed to his later assassination.[30]

5. Reflection Elusiveness

These examples above serve to illustrate how difficult it is in actuality to pursue Machiavelli's prescription of truly, honestly, fairly reflective analysis in a 3D-entrained environment.

Pressing issues of international tension and dispute are thus not necessarily difficult to solve in the abstract, but are often paralyzed by peripherals of bias, prejudice, grudges, and other agendæ - some of which being taboo to openly acknowledge.[31]

If the past is forbidden, the present cannot be completely and correctly understood. The result is that a would-be problem-solver is constrained both by doublethink and thoughtcrime which he cannot see or cannot even mention if he does.

This is the dilemma and tragedy of the existing, PhysWar environment - and it is the actual explanation why ostensible attempts at diplomacy, negotiation, and cooperation inexorably and inevitably disintegrate into

---

[30] Prouty, L. Fletcher, *JFK: The CIA, Vietnam, and the Plot to Assassinate John F. Kennedy*. New York: Carol Publishing Group, 1996.

[31] The United Nations expropriation of Palestine notwithstanding, Israel maintains that its true right to Palestine comes directly from its god, YHVH, through Moses and as established by King David. In inconvenient actuality there is no archæological evidence whatever that Moses ever existed, that there was an Egyptian "exodus", or that Judaic kings named David and Solomon actually existed. Nor is there any evidence of Solomon's legendary Temple; the popular "wailing wall" was never part of any Jewish temple. Cf. Ernest L. Martin, *The Temples that Jerusalem Forgot*. Academy for Scriptural Knowledge, 1994.

PW. Which itself, as shown in *MindWar*, solves nothing, but only perpetuates and deepens the Earth's wounds.

B. 4D Fear

As mentioned above, conventional national and international political analyses are usually strictly 3D, painting a picture of the present situation while stopping short of projecting its future. At most the implications of the continuation of certain current conditions may be identified, but not to the extent of concrete predictions.

Historical factors contributing to the present picture may be cited, but such recitation is not true 4D since it is merely a "construction detail" of the 3D portrait.

4D analysis - projection of the future with or without specified adjustments - is rarely if ever ventured, the assumption being that it is too easy for such specificity to be wrong: The past and present are known summaries based on accepted, endorsed facts, but far too many variables are thought to exist to make the future predictable or controllable.

The consequence of 3D analysis is that decision-makers similarly default into 3D responses, which are intended to have a desired impact **only** on the present situation, changing it towards a more desirable 3D "snapshot". The entire process is one of consecutive static "presents", not a 4D dynamic continuum.

1. Political Nonscience

And also again: The validity of an OU science is established by reliable repetition under laboratory conditions. This is an easy threshold in the physical sciences, wherein the elements of a given experiment are generally easy to identify, isolate, separate, and combine.

It's a different matter in the so-called "social sciences" because of the multitude of factors and the elusiveness of anything resembling a "closed laboratory".

As recounted in one of the companion books in this series *MindStar*: Within the course of Western European civilization, governmental concepts went from ancient theocracies antedating the Hellenistic era to an assortment of theologically-endorsed monarchies (the "Age of Absolutism"), to experiments with various mixtures of human-based "social contracts" following the Reformation/CounterReformation/Enlightenment conflagration marking the onset of the modern era.

Along with these metamorphoses the study of human interaction evolved from ancient religion to Classical philosophy to exhausted rejection of both abstract metaphysical principles and dull post-Enlightenment materialism.

Political Theory/Philosophy dutifully restyled itself **Political Science** as it sought to dissect the institutions of sociopolitics and reduce humanity to functional expressions of them. Hence the academic dominance of **Institutionalism** aka **Structural-Functionalism**.

This tidy descriptive methodology underwent a crisis of inadequacy in the late -19th/early-20th centuries when the sterility of mundane utilitarianism was challenged by spontaneous revivals of Romanticism, which reached their ecstatic apotheosis in the authoritarian orgies of Italian Fascism and German National Socialism.

In the first decade following the "disintoxication" of World War II - intellectual as well as territorial - [surviving] Political Scientists strove to reestablish Institutionalism as the dominant paradigm. Yet it remained suspect for its former failure, and a more

Postmodern [32] fashion, **Behavioralism**, was advanced to contest it.

Throughout the 1960s-70s the Institutionalists and the Behavioralists jousted collegially with one another, occasionally leaving bewildered students [such as the author] wondering whether any actual attention was being paid to politics *per se*. The wave, it seemed, was more important than the water.

2. However ...

Until the 1970s Political Science had remained safely within the 3D of present institutions and/or behavior, with respective appeals to historical precedents to shore up current claims of legitimacy.

Respectable Political Scientists were tacitly in agreement that theirs was **not** an actual science, hence proposals, much less attempts to extend the discipline into 4D "futurism" were greeted with an enthusiasm which could only be described as scant.

In 1974 SUNY/Buffalo Professor Albert Somit violated the sanctuary with his blasphemous anthology *Political Science and the Study of the Future*, which, despite a parade of formidable futurists from multidisciplines and an exhaustive bibliography quite adequate to pedestal

---

[32] **Postmodernism** is typically defined by an attitude of skepticism, irony, or distrust toward grand narratives, ideologies, and various tenets of Enlightenment rationality, including notions of human nature, progress, objective reality & morality, absolute truth, and reason. (*Encyclopædia Brittanica*) I am inclined to hypothesize the Lovecraftian offspring resulting from an abominable tryst of Existentialism and Dadaism.

them altogether, came and went without dislodging either/both of the sacred cows.[33]

Indeed in his Introduction Dr. Somit seemed hesitant to come right out and define what he called "Political Futurism", preferring to shadow-box around various subsets such as societal and environmental trends. Ultimately he fell back on confessing his fear of the subject he was purportedly advancing, and defended it only as a response to that fear:

> There are some skeptics, candor requires me to observe, who would regard [political futurism] as plausible but not persuasive. They believe futurism is a fad which is no more subject to rational explanation than any other fad. No doubt there is some element of truth in this view: Social scientists, and perhaps other academics, are prone to faddism, and it would be naïve to argue that this tendency has been totally inoperative.
> But the objection really misses the point. Even if futurism is largely a fad, the question remains: Why **this** fad rather than another? Furthermore even fads may yield constructive results. It would be unfortunate if those who hold to the faddist explanation permit it to prejudice their assessment of futurism's potential for enlarging our capacity to understand, and perhaps even to direct the course of human events.[34]

In point of fact the "futurism" subculture of the 1970s **was** a fad, along with its fellows such as space-colonization and still-lingering Hippie communal retreats [along with their paranoid counterpart, apocalyptic survivalist enclaves] still right here on Earth. Such

---

[33] Somit, Albert, *Political Science and the Study of the Future*. Hinsdale, Illinois: The Dryden Press, 1974. While Dr. Somit both previously and postviously authored many impressive texts and anthologies exploring various aspects and implications of Political Science, this remarkable heresy seems to have vanished from even used-copy availability. Pity.

[34] *Ibid.*, page #4.

positive and negative fantasies, heralded by prophets such as Gerard K. O'Neill of the space-colonial L5 Society[35] and the irrepressible Timothy Leary, who felt that to properly **go** high one should **be** high: L5 psychedelicized to SMI2LE:[36]

> He'll fly his astral plane,
> Takes you trips around the bay,
> Brings you back the same day,
> Timothy Leary.
>
> He'll take you up, he'll bring you down,
> He'll plant your feet back on the ground.
> He'll fly so high, he'll swoop so low.
> Timothy Leary.[37]

The 1970s' exciting aspirations gradually evaporated in the face of disintoxicating realism: NASA's post-Apollo budget dried up, reducing extraterrestrialism to the relatively-workhorse space shuttle, which was limited to utilitarian military and meteorological tasks; initial

---

[35] https://en.wikipedia.org/wiki/L5_Society

[36] https://en.wikipedia.org/wiki/Timothy_Leary

[37] The Moody Blues, "Legacy of a Mind", 1968.

expectations of civilian use, even passenger-tourism, faded slowly, numbly away.[38]

3. Tools

The methods employed by conventional futurists [including rogue Political Scientists] are as follows:

a. Trend Extrapolation

The most commonly- and effortlessly-used, TE simply selects relevant current trends [in economics, population growth, and similar measurables] and projects them ahead as many years as desired, either lineally or logarithmically as seems appropriate.

The more trends are added to a given projection, presumably the more reliable it will be. Or, if the trends are badly chosen, the less reliable the entire picture.

TE has two principal vulnerabilities:

- Presently-unknown discoveries, inventions, or other outside factors may skew or even

---

[38] In 1976 Paul Kantner and I brainstormed some initial plans for "Project Andromeda", which would have contracted the orbital shuttle to broadcast select Jefferson Starship music worldwide as well as on Andromeda Galaxy M-31 calculated vectors absent the distortions and limitations of Earth's atmosphere.

The equipment would have required relatively little space and energy aboard the shuttle(s).

Project Andromeda went as far as initial correspondence with NASA, but was aborted when civilian shuttle use was preempted.

Project Andromeda was inspired by Kantner's dreams of not just hiring, but hijacking the United States' first starship, in his 1970 Hugo Award-nominated album *Blows Against the Empire*:

https://en.wikipedia.org/wiki/Blows_Against_the_Empire

In the 21st-century "Internet age", of course, worldwide music is commonplace. The interstellar cartographics were resurrected for use in my 1977+ *Star Wars* novel *FireForce*:

http://www.amazon.com/dp/1533264392

obsolesce a present trend, as in cars superseding horses as transportation.

•• A chosen trend may be inaccurately weighted against others, or against non-trend developments such as the outbreak of a PhysWar.

b. Flow-Tree

Alternately called a "flow-chart" or "decision-tree", this is not so much a forecast as a systematic narrowing or elimination of possibilities.

The present is represented as a problem, and possible decisions or actions addressing it are drawn from it. Each such solution brings with it new situations and possible new problems, all of which are consecutively charted.

The idea is that the flaws in impracticalities will be quickly apparent and cause that flow-option to dead-end. The more realistic options continue, either dead-ending further along or surviving the extent of the charted sequence.

This, then, is a way of taking the vague and making it explicit, along with consequences. It also has the advantage of being useful for both individuals and groups, as anyone looking at the diagram can offer modifications to it.

c. Cross-Matrix

This is another "narrowing" technique, and indeed cab be used together with a flow-tree in this function.

All of a problem's components are listed along both the top and one side of a matrix [for example money, population, weather, disease, food, etc.]. Under each factor are listed possible changes to it per decisions which could be taken, such as a 50% increase or decrease of the food supply]. Next the intersection boxes on the matrix are filled in as accurately as possible. For instance a 50% reduction in the food supply intersected with the current population health or disease statistic can be estimated to increase it by an appropriate calculation.

The filled-in intersection boxes can then be valued or color-coded as to proportionate influence. The result is a large, filled-in matrix with a mixture of, say, red/yellow/green intersections. This systematizes the decision-maker's options - ideally as simply of choosing a course of action generating the most green and the least red boxes.

Both flow-tree and cross-matrix devices are so sensible and methodical that one would suppose all important decisions to utilize one or both of them. Unfortunately most decisions don't, being instead the product of vague, unweighted emotions and impulses.

d. Scenarios

The use of scenarios is an exercise in reverse-engineering and is thus very close to FF, falling short of it mostly in its sloppiness.

The decision-maker conjures up a picture of the situation as he would like to see it without its present problem(s).

In the case of the Israel/Palestine antipathy, this might be a one- or two-state solution with both groups coexisting peacefully.

Next the decision-maker juxtaposes this ideal to the present and attempts to come up with courses of action to bridge the two.

While such scenarios are often visualized as ideals, it is rarely the case that the necessary paths to them are worked out, for which, indeed, flow-tree and cross-matrix charting would be useful.

e. Models/Games/Simulations

Another "fad" in certain circles of late-20th-century academia was for an instructor to gather a group of students together, present them with a real-world problem, assign each one a role significant to it (chief of state, military commander, financier, ambassador, etc.), and challenge them to address the situation.

This could be interesting, stimulating and fun, but it rarely translated into an actual policy consensus which could be effectively communicated to the modelers' real-world counterparts.

In the present day its ghost persists in the form of elaborate computer-games and simulations, usually for only one or two players, enabling them to fight/avoid World War III from the convenience and safety of a keyboard.

f. Experts

The simplest of all 3D forecasting approaches is just to summon a person, office, or agency assumed to be an expert on the topic at hand, then allow that expert to identify, narrow, and propose the solution.

While on its face this sounds sensible, its vulnerability is that few experts are truly disinterested: each has a motive of some sort: economic advantage, power hegemony, ideological bias, affection/grudge.

At the onset of the 1962 Cuban Missile Crisis the Kennedys, inexperienced in dealing with the Soviet Union, summoned Dean Acheson to the White House to advise them. Acheson had decades of diplomatic experience, but with the much more primitive and paranoid Soviet Union of Stalin's day. Had his advice been followed now, the crisis would have been locked immediately into inflexible, threatening extremes and the inexorable consequence of war. Fortunately Acheson's rigidity was recognized as anachronistic and rejected.

Another common failing of expertise is that, consciously or otherwise, the decision-maker seeks out experts who will reinforce what is already his bias. He is looking not for objectivity but reassurance and a more elaborate and impressive argument for the desired action.

Nay-sayers aren't invited, or if present will be tuned-out or tokenized "devil's advocates" - as happened to Under Secretary of State George Ball when he opposed Lyndon Johnson's escalation of the Vietnam War.

g. Cycles

Ostensibly the most obscure, least understood, and least used 3D tool, cycles might perhaps be more aptly discussed in Chapter #2. These are major or minor changes in background circumstances which recur over identifiable periods of time, sometimes identically but mostly with evolutionary modifications.

A good example of such a mechanism is the Kondratieff Cycle:

In 1925 Soviet economist Nikolai Kondratieff published his observation that in contemporary industrialized countries the common, international economy surged and subsided in 40-60 year cycles (generally referred to as "Kondratieff Waves").

Since then these cycles have proved reliable enough to continue their use in some economic schools, along with later-formulated "short waves" subsidiary to the "long" KWs.[39]

---

[39] #PR-76-10009, *An Analysis of the Cyclical Dynamics of Industrialized Countries.* Langley, Virginia: Central Intelligence Agency, January 1976.

C. Resources

> I use not only all the brains I have, but also all I can borrow.
>
> > - Woodrow Wilson

Even in conventional, 3D forecasting, the task of identifying, collecting, and correlating all of the material data, often on a worldwide scale, is daunting. Fortunately, the more so in the "Internet Age", numerous instant-access and either free or inexpensive resources exist to facilitate this chore.

Listed here are some of the most practical ones I have found and utilized with impressive objectivity, substance, and reliability.

Most forecasting services today are understandably in the *genre* of economics and marketing, as they exist for commercial purposes.

The ones I have identified here don't ignore economics, but are more principally focused on sociopolitical forecasting.

1. World Future Society

From its website:

> The World Future Society is the world's premier community of future-minded citizens. A 501(c)(3) organization founded in 1966, the organization is driven by three critical objectives:
>
> (1) Uniting people passionate about building their desired futures through an ecosystem of members, chapters and partners.
>
> (2) Advocating to bring to public awareness the world's major challenges. We ignite the futurist mindset in those who no longer want to be bystanders.
>
> (3) Building global labs where futurists of all types are able to produce solutions, that are not solely reactive to the present, but to architect new systems that make the broken ones obsolete.

> Our membership is made up of futurists of all types;
> entrepreneurs, executives, forecasters, economists,
> scientists, students, parents, and conscious citizens. We are
> united by our shared desire to tackle the world's biggest
> challenges.[40]

As perhaps not surprising given its 1960s' inception, WFS is less a directed-research resource than it is an initiation into the hobby & habit of "futurism": contemplating and pursuing one's life with "the future" accented. It's a bit like visiting Disneyland and spending the day in Tomorrowland.

WFS publications don't emphasize alerts and alarms, bur rather on general environments in a "world citizen lifestyle" context. While not deliberately ignoring or concealing unpleasant information, its tone is clearly positive, constructive, and optimistic.

For its first several years WFS had two levels of individual affiliation: "regular" and "academic". The latter was indeed for professionals interested in detailed, directed research. During my graduate studies I found it invaluable, and in those pre-Internet days of the 1970s, both versatile and responsive.

Today there are more-expensive WFS individual memberships, but they appear to principally provide more preferential amenities at WFS events.

2. Stratfor

Stratfor is the most efficient targetable forecasting resource I've found on the Internet as of 2017 publishing time. It provides a mix of both free and subscription services. From its website:

---

[40] http://www.wfs.org

What We Do

As a geopolitical analysis firm, Stratfor provides valuable context to global events that empowers businesses, governments, and individuals to confidently navigate an increasingly complex international environment. Founded 20 years ago around the principle that transformative world events are not random, but are in fact predictable, Stratfor has grown into one of the world's most respected providers of strategic analysis and forecasting.

How We Do It

By leveraging a deep understanding of history, politics and geography along with our unique methodology, Stratfor delivers informed perspectives on today's events and develops a more accurate assessment of the future. Dedicated teams of researchers, analysts and writers distill massive amounts of open-source information each day and examine it through the lens of geopolitics to develop comprehensive, independent, unbiased and nonpartisan analyses. Stratfor analysis cuts through the noise to offer valuable understanding and actionable insights to help our readers succeed.

Why We Do It

Globally engaged individuals, Fortune 500 companies, universities and organizations across an array of industries turn to Stratfor for objective geopolitical analysis and forecasting that reveals the underlying significance and future implications of emerging world events.

Our Methodology

Stratfor's proprietary methodology is our framework to predict the shifts in geopolitical power that shape our world and interpret the significance of today's global events. It combines an understanding of geopolitics, detailed analysis and rigorous internal debate, which is then refined into a unified Stratfor perspective. Our analysts begin with a flood of open-source information, filter out the noise, unearth emerging paradigms, challenge assumptions and reconcile conflicting truths to produce actionable analysis and forecasts.[41]

3. Hudson Institute

One of the older and more venerable forecasting enterprises is the Hudson Institute - very much like Stratfor in its scope and sophistication, but more of an academic institution on its own terms - internally-prioritized and generated publications and analyses rather than external user-driven. Still its sophistication and reputation remain impeccable.

I'd recommend Hudson as a more in-depth backup to Stratfor, assuming that it happens to have made detailed studies of your topic of special interest,

> Founded in 1961 by strategist Herman Kahn, Hudson Institute challenges conventional thinking and helps manage strategic transitions to the future through interdisciplinary studies in defense, international relations, economics, health care, technology, culture, and law.
>
> Hudson seeks to guide public policy makers and global leaders in government and business through a vigorous program of publications, conferences, policy briefings, and recommendations.[42]

4. United States Government

The advantage of U.S. Government resources is that they **are** USGr: packed with information, obtained and continuously updated through worldwide bureaucracies, and blessed with essentially-unlimited budgets. Their websites abound with this information, usually free for the viewing & downloading.

---

[41] https://www.stratfor.com

[42] http://www.hudson.org

The disadvantage of USGr is **also** that they are USGr, with their information compiled and published to be in support of Government/current Administration policies, interpretations, and objectives. This shouldn't be taken to mean that the analysts in question are biased or myopic - just that they understand and approach their primary responsibility as supporting U.S. policy rather than objectively critiquing it.

For specialized forecasting in related subjects such as finance and military, it's useful to consult the websites of the most directly-relevant Executive Departments, as in these examples Commerce and Defense.

For more general information, particularly with a political focus, the two most useful are the Department of State and the Central Intelligence Agency.

a. Department of State

The Department of State website has an extensive library of sociopolitical resources, cross-related by various geographic areas, specific nations, non-national ethnic and religious groups, and other classifications.[43] These are identified and accessed by drop-down menus of the website, which efficiently narrow the user's search.

b. Central Intelligence Agency

Contrary to its popular image as a behind-the-Green-Door tree-fort, the Central Intelligence Agency both publishes and makes websearch-available vast quantities of information [at the Unclassified level]. Per its website:

> The CIA releases millions of pages of documents each year and frequently releases items of public interest on this website. The Library contains a wealth of information, from

---

[43] https://www.state.gov

unclassified current publications to basic references, reports and maps.

The *World Factbook* provides information on the history, people, government, economy, geography, communications, transportation, military, and transnational issues for 267 world entities. Our Reference tab includes: maps of the major world regions, as well as Flags of the World, a Physical Map of the World, a Political Map of the World, a World Oceans map, and a Standard Time Zones of the World map. [44]

It should be added that both DOS and CIA also attempt to be responsive to public requests for specialized information, and not just within Freedom of Information Act (FOIA) formalities. Simply send them a letter with your question of interest, and you may be surprised by the materials it elicits. [45]

---

[44] https://www.cia.gov/library

[45] Sometimes this occurs with James Bond melodramatics. Some years ago I wrote to the CIA asking for any information they might have on Kondratieff Cycles. About a month later I received a copy of an extensive CIA report, with the envelope's return-address that of a gentleman in Arlington, VA. When I wrote to thank him, my letter was returned as "undeliverable". As I later discovered, both the person and the address were fictitious CIA blinds.

Chapter 4: Phases, Layers, & Dimensions

The Three Laws of MindWar

1. MindWar is the conduct of war without injury or death to human beings, and without the disruption or destruction of their means of livelihood.

2. While MindWar includes access to the human mind, this is done only to stimulate its capacity for and interest in cooperative problem-solving.

3. PhysWar is the consequence of MindWar failure. Therefore MindWar must not be allowed to fail.[46]

A. MindWar Interlocks

As introduced in *MindWar* and expanded herein, a MW campaign addressed to a given problem situation is completely alien to conventional PhysWar reactive flailing. PW **invariably** fails, and fails with substantial destruction, affliction, and loss-of-life, because it is inherently a desperate, last-resort reaction to similarly-haphazard diplomacy: ultimately a series of *ad hoc* bandages applied, too little/too late, to a widening social

---

[46] Aquino, Michael A., *MindWar*. San Francisco: Barony of Rachane, 2016, page #38.

wound. In the idiom of FF, it is a succession of disconnected 3D artifices.

The same national or international environment under MW vigilance ideally never permits a wound to develop in the first place. MW resources' intelligence anticipates potential disequilibrium and adjusts it back to stability before the ordinary humans involved are even aware of any potential disruption.

Thus the majority of MW solutions in effect apply solutions preempting their associated problems.

B. MW Resources

1. The MindWar TriForce

As detailed in *MindWar* Part II, the United States' MW capability is concentrated in three United States Army MW Branches, evolved from the old Special Operations Forces: **MetaForce**/MFB (superseding Special Forces/SF), **MindWar**/MWB (superseding Psychological Operations/PO), and **ParaPolitics**/PPB (superseding Civil Affairs/CA).

Despite transparent efforts to cosmeticize them, all three of the obsolete Branches functioned *de facto* as "battlefield janitors", tasked with cleaning up the mess left by PW combat Branches' death and destruction.

These three renewed Branches are designed to function both independently and in concert with one another, throughout the [up to] four Phases of a MW campaign.

2. The PhysWar Branches

Importantly and crucially, the MW Special Operations TriForce is the **primary and exclusive** deployment presence of the United States in a failed-diplomacy crisis situation.

The PW Branches remain in stand-down, as a "contingency threat" only. In this role they may be paraded, brandished in displays and "war games", and otherwise showcased as may lend additional enthusiasm for and cooperation with the MW campaign, but any actual use of their destructive capabilities is absolutely prohibited.

In this role the PW weaponry becomes treated, and regarded, with exactly the same foreboding as nuclear capabilities since Hiroshima and Nagasaki: They are taken utterly seriously, but their actual use is never considered an actual option.

In a pre-campaign environment ("Phase Ø"), geographically-assigned MFB teams remain alert for imbalances. If such occurs and cannot be rebalanced through the actions of one or more MFB teams, the mental-conditioning technologies of MWB are introduced to condition the affected humans towards greater receptivity to the MFB efforts. While in a Phase Ø mode, these processes are completely invisible: not so much clandestine as quietly unnoticed. MF teams are constituted to blend in seamlessly with local races and cultures, while the MWB Psychological Controls (PSYCONs) are predominantly activated from remote distances to target the subconscious functions of the human brain.[47]

As its designation connotes, Phase Ø is, like an ordinary PW environment, one of 3D stasis. There is no need for 4D dynamics until/unless destabilization reaches a severity and inertia requiring the declaration of a MW campaign (Phases 1-4).

---

[47] The 14 principal PSYCONs are detailed in *MindWar* Chapter #3.

C. MW Declaration

If MW Phase Ø monitoring fails to preserve equilibrium, and a policy decision is taken to actively resolve the disequilibrium, then a MW campaign is formally commenced and Phase 1 initiated.

As prescribed in *MindWar*, a MW campaign begins with the formality of a "Declaration of MW".[48]

1. PW-Era *Status Quo*

a. PW Declarations

In conventional PhysWars (PW) such Declarations, when antagonists even bother with them, have been emotional, angry accusations of grievances along with the stated intent to respond to them by PW violence. The supposed goal of such PW is not part of the Declaration.

Indeed throughout recorded history the dismaying fact is that PWs have **never** known where they would be going once declared; such bothersome details were impatiently brushed aside in the passion of the commencement, for others to grapple with later, assuming anyone survived with the acumen and resources necessary to do so.

Perhaps the sole, and underappreciated exception to this was the practice of Imperial Rome to announce its campaigns to a decided enemy, and even more importantly to convey the inevitability of Roman victory in the undertaking. As Livy observed:

> The terror of the Roman name will be such that the world shall know that, once a Roman army has laid siege to a city, **nothing** will move it - not the rigors or winter nor the weariness of months and years - that it knows no end but

---

[48] *Ibid.*, page #184.

victory and is ready, if a swift and sudden stroke will not serve, to preserve until that victory is achieved.[49]

The effect of this perception obviously went far beyond the battle or war of the moment; it was a major deterrent to provocations of the Empire, contributing to the famous - and never-repeated - *Pax Romana*. The Xth Legion's 375' earthen ramp, constructed in 73 C.E. to the "unassailable" Judæan fortress of Masada, remains to this day a mute, stark testimony to this implacable determination.[50]

b. PW NonDeclarations

Since aggressive PW was *pro forma* outlawed upon the post-World War II founding of the United Nations, it is no longer "politically correct" to baldly aggress. Hence aggressor nations, including as so-inclined the United States, couch PW Declarations as defensive responses to unprovoked belligerence.[51]   If a suitably-outrageous

---

[49] Keller, Werner, *The Etruscans*. New York: Alfred A. Knopf, 1974, page 262.

[50] Glorified Hollywood revisionism notwithstanding, the Sicari rebels who seized Masada in 70 C.E. first massacred its Roman garrison, then wreaked havoc in the countryside, including slaughtering 700 women and children in the nearby village of Ein Gedi. In 73 the Roman Governor Lucius Flavius Silva personally led the Xth Legion to put a stop to the terror. When Silva breached Masada, he found that the Sicari had killed themselves and any who refused suicide: 960 men, women, and children in all. Only two women and five children were found alive. Cf. "Masada", Wikipedia for multiple sources.

[51] All Members shall refrain in their international relations from the threat or use of force against the territorial integrity or political independence of any state, or in any other manner inconsistent with the Purposes of the United Nations. - *United Nations Charter*, Article 2, ¶4.

incident is not ready-to-hand, an appropriate false-flag operation is duly executed and bewailed.

c. False-Flag

False-flags are covert attacks staged so as to appear conducted by a nation or group other than oneself. They are used to attack one's own territory & people, or others' for whom one wishes to falsify actual responsibility.

As George Orwell indifferently observed in *1984*, domestic populations emotionally reject believing that their own governments would kill some or even many of them merely to excuse attacking a foreign target. Such is appallingly not just routine, but unremarkably so.[52]

2. MW-Era *Status Post*

a. "Enemy" Definition

The MW contrast to this shameless, shameful PW *danse macabre* could not be more diametrically its repudiation.

Most essentially and immediately, humans are **not** harmed nor their property destroyed, because they are **never** defined as "the enemy".[53]

Rather the enemy is **the problem situation itself**, against which **all** involved humans are in alliance to overcome.

---

[52] "The Horror ... the Horror ..." - Colonel Walter E. Kurtz (Marlon Brando), U.S. Army Special Forces, in Francis Ford Coppola's *Apocalypse Now* (1979).

[53] This includes the armed forces of other interventionists, regardless which government or faction they may be supporting. A MW campaign blankets **all** humans, including one's own forces, with the same MW PSYCONs. It is thereby that the desired cooperative atmosphere is created among all participants.

b. Transparency

MW is thus a completely cooperative effort, and as such is prosecuted equally-completely in the open: Neither its intelligence, planning, or execution is concealed or Classified.

When *MindWar* first appeared in 2013, this brazen transparency elicited instinctive consternation among strategists indoctrinated and seasoned in operational secrecy. MW seemed glaringly, indeed blasphemously counterintuitive. Upon reflection the logic overcame the knee-jerk: Consideration of the **entire** range of human perspective concerning a given problem is required for an equally-comprehensive solution: composition rather than imposition.

c. Phase 1 Diagnostics

The principal activity of Phase 1 is, thus cooperatively, to thoroughly identify and diagnose the "disease", **not** its symptoms.

Here too the difference from PW is dramatic, since PW invariably focuses on the **expressions** and **consequences** such as civil disturbances and armed revolts, and directs its energies towards suppressing them.

MW, on the other hand, focuses on such eruptions' **underlying causes**, through a sequential, layered application of diagnostics, culminating in the campaign-activating **Foundation Diagnosis** (FD).

d. Foundation Diagnosis

The final and most comprehensive in a progressive series of situation diagnostics in Phase 1 of a MindWar campaign.

The FD is so-named in tribute to Dr. Isaac Asimov's "psychohistory"[54] *Foundation* novels, the FD takes initial form in a 3D research & analysis process, but then, and crucially, becomes 4D dynamic as it is progressively modified throughout the subsequent three Phases of the MW campaign.

Unsurprisingly it is the completed 3D Phase 1 FD which is formalized and published as the **Declaration of MW**. It defines the problem situation in its totality, focusing upon its underlying causes. It identifies the combined national, factional, and/or individual human interest and participation in a campaign to overcome it.

Finally it [preliminarily] outlines the standards according to which the campaign's success will be measured in-progress and finally achieved upon MW victory.

Further unlike the haphazard blindness of PW Declarations, a MW Declaration is conceived and constructive to be inevitable and irresistible. It is a course of action which not only takes all variables into account, but establishes their pre-control and constant adjustment during the campaign, never allowing their inertia to exceed that of the campaign.

Thus the Third Law of MW - **that it cannot be allowed to fail** - is not mere hyperbole: It is absolutely, uncompromisingly in earnest.

---

[54] **Psychohistory**: That branch of mathematics which deals with the reactions of human conglomerates to fixed social and economic stimuli. Implicit in this definition is the assumption that the human conglomerate being dealt with is sufficiently large for valid statistical treatment. A further necessary assumption is that the human conglomerate be itself unaware of psychohistorical analysis in order that its reactions be truly random. - Isaac Asimov, *Foundation*, 1951

D. Dual-Direction

1. Obverse: *Áristos*

In Phase 2 of a MW campaign, the 3D Phase 1 FD/ Declaration initially constructed by the MetaForce (MF) research & analysis assets, with later augmentation by corresponding teams and PSYCONs from the MindWar Branch (MWB) begins its translation into the campaign's dynamic, 4D continuum.

The 4D directional goal MFB & MWB develop is the necessary consequence and culmination of the campaign: the *áristos* - the "best possible practical solution".

Referring back to Chapter #1, this is Machiavelli's combination of *virtu* and *occasione*, resulting in *ordini*. It would be quite possible to limit the MW campaign to this implicit practicality, and indeed in certain cases limitations caused by external factors such as time, logistics, MW resources, or the intrusion/complication of other problems may dictate this conservatism.

2. Reverse: *Kalokagathia*

Ideally, however, a MW campaign addresses its outcome 4D bidirectionally. Complementing the forward-projecting *áristos* is a reverse-projected ideal outcome, corresponding to Machievelli's vision of *civitas*. This is the "best imaginable" outcome, comprising a "clean sheet of paper" or "from the ground up" redesign of the target national, community, geographic area, or other demarcation of the MW campaign scope. Thus Machiavelli's *civitas* corresponds to Plato's ideal of *kalokagathia*.[55]

---

[55] Cf. Chapter #1.B.

3. ParaPolitics Branch

Conception and construction of this ideal, however, is not utopian daydreaming: It requires a methodical approach, and a correspondingly-expert authority to exercise it.

This operation is the responsibility of the third component of the MW Special Operations TriForce: ParaPolitics Branch (PPB).

As developed in *MindWar* Chapter #5, PPB is the evolutionary successor to the PW-era Civil Affairs Branch, a "battlefield janitor" element relegated to cleaning up the carnage, destruction, and life-support devastation left in the wake of PW combat operations.

In a MW campaign, of course, such a catastrophic disintegration is never allowed to occur. The preemptive and adjusting activities of MFB & MWB stabilize the situation before it has a chance to devolve to that state.

However the purpose of a MW campaign is not just to secure such stability, nor even to perpetuate it per *áristos*; it is to **perfect** it - or, more precisely, to establish a self-perfecting *polis*.

4. *Agathon*

PPB's point of planning departure (which happens also to be its point of ultimate future arrival) is not a governmental, political, or social structure *per se*, but rather an all-encompassing centerpiece of **morality**: in Platonic terminology the *Agathon*.[56]

To illustrate and elaborate:

> The most stable, civilized, and pleasant societies of antiquity - such as Egypt, Crete, and Hellenic Greece - share a surprisingly simple, yet subsequently forgotten principle: that of **a polis defined, united, and energized by a common moral principle**.
>
> In Egypt this was the cosmic principle or *neter* (god/goddess) of *Maat*, usually simplified as "justice" but more precisely extending to virtue, fairness, and rectitude in all personal and community affairs. There was no concept of individual rights against the government, because government was viewed as a system ordered by the *neteru*. Similarly each Egyptian, whether high- or low-born, participated in this system. Crime and corruption were of course possible, but inadvisable because of the conviction that vice would be punished severely after Earthly death.
>
> Virtue in Mesopotamia was understood as obedience to the willful desires of the god(s), not harmony with their natural principles. The "wrath of the gods" was feared by the state in Mesopotamia, as it was never in Egypt (which was ruled by a god-king). The Mesopotamian king sought the "right ruling" of his community, in accordance with the Akkadian principle of *Shulmu* (later adopted by the Hebrews as *Shalom*): a term meaning not just "peace" but the community well-being that engenders peace.
>
> Hellenic Greece includes the civilizations of Crete (b. 2700 BCE), Greece (Mycenæ b. 1600 BCE, Athens b. 600 BCE), the Ægean islands, and Magna Græcia (Sicily and southern Italy). The Hellenic Greek cultures are most notable for exalting the intellect - for making the universe an

---

[56] In classical political thought there was a concern to locate authority beyond anything that anyone could appropriate, either in wisdom or in justice, or, as in the Platonic *Agathon* - the supreme Good which is beyond definition. The *Agathon* can accommodate as many formulations as there are human beings, and every person can make his own report. As there will always be a transcending or conceivable Good beyond the good(s) of particular individuals, the *Agathon* is ineffable and indefinable, and necessarily transcends the spatial and temporal limits of finite powers of perception. - Iyer, Raghavan N., *ParaPolitics: Toward the City of Man*. New York: Oxford University Press, 1979, page #22.

intelligible tool and/or puzzle for mankind to explore, understand, and use. They did not conceive mankind as having a "mission" from the gods, though the gods could influence human fortunes for good or ill. To the extent that the Greeks put humanity at the "center" of importance, they worshipped its body (as in athletics and the Olympic Games) and its mind (as in the sophistic and philosophical schools of Athens).

The Cretan (Minoan) political system, a bureaucratic monarchy most significant for its peacefulness, included no evident slavery, standing military, or marked class distinctions. Women appear to have been politically equal with men. The Minoan culture was destroyed ca. 1400 BCE by an invasion from Mycenæ. The Mycenæan culture, which faded into the Greek "dark ages" within another three centuries, denied women equality and did have slavery.

The "dark ages" lasted from 1100 to 800 BCE and came to an end with the founding of the first Greek city-states. The first Greek writing appears in about the 8th century BCE, with the first dated writing in 600 BCE.

The later Hellenic era (600-300 BCE) - based as it was on empirical investigation and inductive reasoning - was a challenge to the older, tribal way of doing things. Previously custom (*nomos*) was the rule for behavior, and to follow custom was *dike*, the path of justice. Disregard of custom was *hybris* and was unacceptable and even dangerous beyond its immediate implications.

As it became increasingly evident that social problems, such as the reform of Athenian laws by Draco and then Solon, could be solved by either an appeal to either relative practicality or absolute standards, a growing controversy arose concerning the relation of *nomos* to *physis* (nature or the divine order). Foremost of the absolutists was Pythagoras, who sought in number the beginning or *arche* of things - the ordering principle or "one behind the many".[57]

Even a cursory glance around the contemporary Western international community reveals that nowhere is such a transcendent, metaphysical *Agathon* to be found.

---

[57] *MindWar, op. cit.*, pages #157-9.

True, the post-Enlightenment[58] West pretends generally to Christian morality, but in actuality this is merely a ceremonial veneer: services, blessings, invocations, and platitudes which have absolutely no force in implemented public affairs. Every now and then the Roman Catholic pope makes an appeal for some moral sanctimony, which is popularly acclaimed and then immediately ignored.

E. PW-Era *Status Quo*

Today there are only two principal metaethical systems influencing actual national operation: Judaism in the state of Israel and Islam in the several nations subordinating themselves to various interpretations of this theology.

This accordingly makes both Israel and the Islamic world "irrational" in Western eyes, hence mysteriously threatening.

The United States resolves this in the case of Israel by accepting and obeying it unquestioningly, an in the case of Islam by ignoring it [among useful allies, such as Saudi Arabia] or PW-attacking it [elsewhere].

Correspondingly both Israel and Islam regard the *de facto*-atheistic West generally, and the United States especially, as "godless" and decadent.

A curious "third theocracy" existed for most of the 20th Century in the form of ideological communism, or more precisely the "denominations" of Marxism, Marxism-Leninism, and Maoism. Each of these avowed a "god" prior to and preemptive of ethical relativism: most

---

[58] As specifically discussed here, the European "Enlightenment" (late 17th-18th Centuries) was an intellectual revolt against the church-proclaimed **metaethics** of Christianity in favor of purely-utilitarian reason: **ethical relativism**. However such judgments were still reserved to sovereigns; thus murder is acceptable, even admirable if prescribed by a state, but proscribed & punishable in the individual.

generally the economic class stratification and warfare of Marx & Engels. This "god", which could only be obeyed, not ignored or dethroned, is technically called **dialectic materialism** in contrast to the **dialectic idealism** of Georg Hegel, which posited a similar, albeit deistic "god-dictated" social evolution in the "lives" of nation-states.[59]

At this 2017 writing god-communism is no more: discarded by Russia and its former European satellites ca. 1989 and corrupted into a cynical state-capitalism in remnant-alcoves such as China and Vietnam.

F. MW-Era *Status Post*

This, then, is the *tableau* which PPB confronts when considering the achievable necessity for the *Agathon* in [para]political perfectionism:

1. Theistic States

In the case of Israel and Islamic nations/groups, a supreme superstitions exist but are nowhere near the purity and nobility of a true *Agathon*.

Before PPB can undertake to actualize *kalokagathia* in these cases, it will be necessary to annihilate and replace the existing monstrosity with a pure *Agathon* in the same imagery. This task is assigned to MWB, whose

---

[59] The inevitable, ominous apotheosis of dialectic idealism was the Romantic deification of the state as realized in Italian Fascism and German National Socialism. This completely submerged and absorbed individual human life into the "living state", which thereby asserted an absolute right to strengthen and perpetuate itself: which aspiration constituted its entire "morality". In the non-communist West the human alienation this inspired led to the post-World War II rejection of Hegelian metaphysics generally, and the ascent of such anti-ideologies as European Existentialism and the American Beat Generation.

PSYCONs can be used to accomplish this substitution without the conscious awareness of affected humans.

2. Atheistic States

In the case of the materialist West, the task of generating an Agathon again falls to MWB, but this time its orientation and azimuth are significantly different: The dormant, disdained "spirit of mankind" - Plato's recognition in the *Republic* that humanity "unchained from the darkness of the cave" will aspire to the light of *Agathon*. Once again this is not to be attempted at the conscious, rational level of targeted humans, but subconsciously through MWB's PSYCONs. The pleasant result will be a new perception of and insistence upon the *Agathon* at all socioeconomic levels, eclipsing the cold, dead numbness of the PW-era cultural climate.

3. External Harmonization

It is of course a relatively incidental but nonetheless essential matter to coordinate such MWB projects so that the *Agathon* as created in all of the above environments not only fulfills the needs and controls the superstitions or substitute-superstitions of the directly-affected human groups, but also integrates smoothly and constructively into the external international community. That community will most likely not understand the localized mechanism or the reasons for it, nor be susceptible to the PSYCONs employed.

G. *Agathon*: Key to *Kalokagathia*

The importance of this step in PPB's *kalokagathia* project **cannot be overemphasized**. Indeed once the *Agathon* is established and in force, the remaining

Phases of the MW campaign rather fall easily into place as though "magnetized". Once the MWarrior understands and applies the above principles and preparations, there will be neither surprise nor mystery to this "waterfall".

H. Pyramid of the *Agathon*

Indeed we're not ready to leave the *Agathon* just yet.

As is doubtless clear from the above discussion, it's an essential principle. Everything depends upon it, which means that it must be correctly perceived and apprehended.

This further necessitates explaining it coherently and meaningfully to humans who will both apply it at higher levels of *polis* responsibility and be affected by it at lower levels.

1. PW-Era *Status Quo*

Consider the ostensibly-simplistic example of the Judæo-Christian God as utilized in a non-MW environment:

At the highest, control level of the various institutional churches and synagogues, God is identified and represented as an abstraction beyond human comprehension. As such it is not personified, nor is any effort made to communicate with it. It is simply, and only, posited to exist.

From this insistence religious policy-makers decide in what ways it can be useful to them, and speak, write, and/ or act on its behalf accordingly. If Aquinas' Divine Law revelation is claimed, this is the level at which it will be asserted as a policy lynchpin, as for instance Catholic Papal "infallibility".

Lower-tier clerics and executives are not permitted to challenge these representations, on the grounds that they are not sufficiently intelligent, educated, or sophisticated to understand, much less critique them. Or simply that they are not sufficiently purified to receive Divine Law revelations.

Also at progressively-lower levels, God is transformed from an abstraction to a personification: an old man with a white beard, a burning bush, a pillar of fire, or whatever else serves control purposes. Family (Mary, Jesus, *et al.*), a support staff (angels), and mischief-makers (Satan & dæmons) are added where they may be encouragingly or coercively useful.

Over the centuries a complete and versatile mythology encompassing all of these is assembled, appropriated from other religions, and modified to remain relevant and effective as a control device among progressive human cultures and generations. The overall result ranges from an ever-more-abstract metaphysical ideology at the top to an easy-to-understand comic book at the bottom. Within this collective everyone gets what he needs, and what keeps him docile and obedient.

2. MW-Era *Status Post*

With the MW *Agathon* it's another matter entirely. Instead of being a whimsical fantasy of convenience which is pushed downward for purposes of control and exploitation, approaching the *Agathon* begins at the most elementary levels of human consciousness, thence is progressively refined to ever-more-exacting elaborations, until a final, perfect apprehension is attained.

3. The Pyramid[60]

---

[60] Iyer, Raghavan, *ParaPolitics*. New York: Oxford University Press, 1979, page #48.

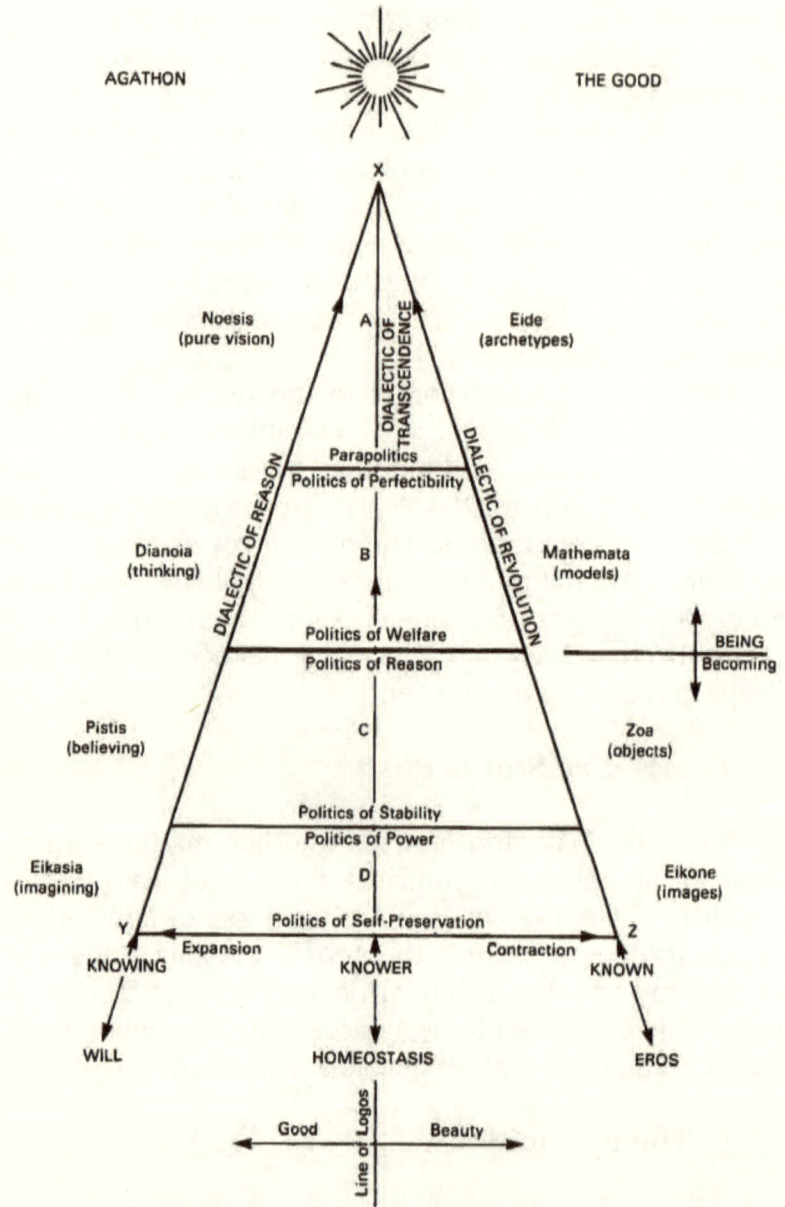

If the reader is unused to his thoughts being dissected with such terrifying exactitude, it is not surprising given the habitual *eikasia* of conventional, PW-conditioned humanity. With correlation to the "Thought Architecture" analysis in *MindWar*, however, this bewildering diagram becomes quite straightforward and intelligible.[61]

a. Thought Architecture

As detailed in *MindWar* and retouched upon in Chapter #2 of this book, human thought overall consists of **consciousness** and **subconsciousness**, of which the latter is by far the more active (95%) and influential.

In individual human experience, however, these are not perceived as hard-and-fast separations; they blend into one other without notice or concern. [Indeed they are frequently difficult to distinguish outside of a laboratory environment.]

b. Below the Base

When initially considering the Pyramid, note that below it is "homeostasis", which is the state of mind at rest. [When this methodology is applied to a political situation or object (such as a nation, culture, or group), it is the existing state of affairs.]

Absent application of the Pyramid, conventional, PW-level individuals or institutions know and undertake nothing more than attempting to balance an arbitrary standard of "good" (usually a superficial ideology) with "beauty" (behavior at least somewhat responsive to it).

This is the balance, such as it is, that can be seen in all PW-environment diplomacies, and which is supposedly, if rarely actually, the PW-goal when the diplomacy fails.

---

[61] *MindWar, op. cit.*, pages #81-5.

c. Conscious Ascent

Now in the capacity of a PPB MWarrior rise to the Pyramid of *Agathon*.

The **left**-side ascending-line is labeled "Dialectic of Reason". The term *dialectic* (ancient Greek διαλεκτική) refers to the establishment of a philosophical truth by the means of rigorous, cooperative discourse, whereby the reconciliation of two or more perspectives yields a more accurate one.

Therefore the left-side ascending line shows an increasing resolution of conscious thought from *Eikasia* (primitive impulse) to *Pistis* (ordinary active/reactive sensations & decisions) to *Dianoia* (precise, logical, reflection[62]), and finally [possibly, potentially] to *Nœsis* (intuition and apprehension [of the *Agathon*]).

Note that this entire progression rests upon a "foundation" of **will**: that is, a deliberate effort at all levels is required to actualize it.

d. Subconscious Ascent

The **right**-side ascending line addresses the subconscious elements of the thought-experience.

It rests upon a base of ***eros***, which refers to a sentient being's obsessive passion for the truth. [Ultimately this stems from any such being's bewilderment at its own "unexplained" existence and compulsion to discover that explanation.]

This desire initially results in random, generalized images, identified here as *eikone* ("icons"), which, as they grow stronger and more continuous, coalesce into *zoa* (objects).

---

[62] Cf. Chapter #1.

As these sensations increase in composition and clarity, they are further realized as built-up complexities (*mathemata*).

Penultimately separate models form the basis for *eide* (archetypes), which serves to distinguish the permanent from the transitory: realization of the [Platonic] Forms, the [Egyptian] *neteru*.

The entire right-side ascent dynamic is called the "Dialectic of Revolution" in that it is goal-, not process-driven [as contrasted to the conscious "Reason"].

e. Convergence

As the pyramid-shape illustrates, with each increase in refinement, definition, and focus, the distance between the conscious and the subconscious narrows; at the apex they are completely unified into a single identity.

f. Transcent

There is also a **central** ascending line - the "Dialectic of Transcendence" - which represents the intended purpose of the entire thought: the apprehension of its "governing" *Agathon*.

[For the time being the several "crossbars" of "Politics of -" may be set aside, as they are better-clarified below.]

Admission to the Dialectic of Transcendence is not casual or trivial; as shown at its point of entry, it requires the key of *logos*.

The ancient Greeks saw the Objective Universe (OU) divided into a non-conscious, automatic functioning (*physis*) conceived and implemented by a divine intelligence and consciousness (*logos*).

The individual human intelligence (*nous*) was capable of coherent recognition and application of the *logos*; each human was thus a microcosm of the macrocosmic *logos*. As Raghavan Iyer relates:

> In classical Greece the term *nomos* had to do with measure. As early as Sophocles, *agraphos nomos*, the unwritten law, had divine sanction, and with the later Stoics it was grounded in nature (*physis*) as the immanent *logos*.
>
> *Nous* for Anaxagoras was both a cosmological principle as the source of all motion, and an immanent principle in all living beings.
>
> Diogenes qualified the principle, which he denominated *ær-nous*, by replacing mechanistic interpretations with the view that its activity is intelligent and forms the best possible *kosmos*, and it is expressed in the operation of a principle of measure among all things.
>
> In the later writings of Plato *kosmos nœtos*, the intelligible universe, is both produced and ordered by *nous*, which is inherent in all men.
>
> Plotinus drew the implication that *nous* is transcendent as the cause of *kosmos nœtos* and is immanent in human beings, each of whom is therefore a *kosmos nœtos*.
>
> The Stoics concluded that the human *nous* is a manifestation of cosmic *nous*.
>
> *Nous* represents a binding-together of human minds as rays from one central source of cosmic intelligence.[63]

Thus as shown the *logos* enables the human intelligent consciousness (*nous*) to transcend the OU (*physis*) by entering into that Dialectic leading to apprehension of the *Agathon*.

---

[63] *ParaPolitics, op. cit.*, pages #54-55.

g. Apprehension

Significantly [and perhaps annoyingly!] the entire Pyramid is not capstoned by the desired *Agathon*. Instead that Grail glows like a star **above** the apex. Why?

Because while all three dialectics are progressive refinements in their respective realms, an authentic *Agathon* is not in any sense a built-up composite. It is a *neter-*/Form-manifestation, hence is **metaphysical**.

What is accomplished by "ascending the Pyramid" is the clearing-away of all impediments to beholding the *Agathon*; it is an authentically divine ecstasy. Indeed for a true *Agathon* it could not be otherwise.

If this all sounds a bit *outré* as a mission-statement for a U.S. Army Branch, it must be remembered what a formidable mission PPB **has**: to ascertain, articulate, and implement the subject *polis'* supreme guiding **morality-principle** (= *Agathon*).

Moreover if it fails in this, the MW campaign must be limited to only the continuum of a dynamic, constantly-adjusting *áristos*. It will not enjoy the permanent and transcendent stability that *kalokagathia* instils.

I. *Kalokagathia* ParaPolitics

Apprehension of an *Agathon* as identified to be ideal for the supercontrol of a given political situation, while the necessary first step, is obviously not going to conclusively solve the problem.

For that PPB needs to first reconceptualize, then methodically promulgate a new *polis* based upon that *Agathon*.

1. PW-Era *Status Quo*

The conventional sequel to PW invasion, destruction, and occupation of a problem situation is styled "nation-building", frequently preceded by the methodical, complete obliteration of the defeated governmental structure.

The imposed replacement puppet government is assembled from local collaborationists and/or obedient, opportunistic exiles, and given a hastily-thrown-together administration structure modeled on Western notions of representative social-contract governments, habitually in the American or British model.

The title "president", with "prime minister" a close second, has become ubiquitous to the point of slapstick in such charades.

A veneer of legitimacy is sometimes added by the staging of "popular elections" wherein, under the ever-present fear of the occupier's or puppet's guns, the masses are herded to cast ballots for one or two pre-approved candidates. Such elections are routinely rigged, and in the rare instance of an upstart result, the victor is discarded by re-election, *coup*, or deportation.

It hardly needs observing that this is no way to remedy post-PW devastation. Probably the most compelling example is the rise of Nazi Germany in eventual response to the national punishment, exploitation, and hypocrisy inflicted by the Versailles Treaty. Since then the catalogue of repeat-performances has been unending, leading to the contemporary international community's omnipresent instability.

Recent examples include the 2013 military removal of the post-revolutionary elected Egyptian President Mohammed Morsi (sentenced to death in 2015 for emphasis) and the 2014 [unconstitutional] parliamentary dismissal of Ukrainian President Viktor Yanuyovch for favoring economic ties closer to Russia than the European Union.

With no viable PW-era reform on the horizon, the 21st Century has seen a worldwide surge in population instability characterized by disinterest in government participation, material/economic rather than ideological individual motivations, and increasing migration to anywhere that promises greater such opportunities and advantages.

"Patriotism" is increasingly disdained by political dissidents as anachronistic propaganda for the PW-enslavement of the stupid and naïve.

2. MW-Era *Status Post*

It would be too much to expect for MW to miraculously reform a planet gripped in PW-convulsion.

What **can** be commenced are incremental cures. Directly and immediately these benefit the afflicted local humans; possibly they also serve as example for others to emulate in whole or part, even absent the impetus of a collapse in the existing structure.

Following on from the above discussion of the *Agathon*, it should be immediately obvious that PPB's approach to *polis*-initiation has absolutely nothing in common with PW heavy-handedness.

From the beginning PPB teams meld with the local populace at all social, economic, ethnic, and cultural levels. It is PPB's initial function to expose this collective to the previously-apprehended *Agathon*, in graduated metaphors enabling all to understand and recognize it at their level of intelligence, education, and life-discretion.

At this stage, which generally corresponds to MW campaign Phase 2, MWB is a constant, omnipresent, invisible presence through application of a tailored PSYCON mix blanketing the entire geographic area.

The result of this is not some kind of sinister "brainwashing" after the fashion of PW-era "re-education" torture, but simply a general stimulation of individual energy, cognitive awareness, and amicable cooperation.

As detailed in *MindWar*, the MWB PSYCONs operate predominantly at the subconscious level; in effect they serve to jump-start the "right side" of the *Agathon* Pyramid - which, with its 95% Thought Architecture presence, practically enables the Pyramid's rational "left side" to harmonize near-effortlessly.

Once again such a rosy picture is not hyperbolic fantasy. It is based upon the very real, very scientific, and very demonstrable MW principles introduced and substantiated herein and in *MindWar*; and wherever actualized will quickly be validated by results. All that is required is the vision and the will to do it.

And remember that MW is not a "zero-sum game"; if it is not attempted, the PW alternative will continue to fill the vacuum.

3. ParaPolitics Components

Designing and implementing the *Agathon*-inspired *polis* requires the identification and tailoring of several political factors and functions, collectively entitled "ParaPolitics" by Dr. Raghavan Iyer, who extensively an exhaustively described them in his 1979 book of that title.

Once again these are most easily seen and correlated in diagram:[64]

---

[64] *ParaPolitics, op. cit.*, page #26. The hexagram is employed simply to interrelate the named concepts, and does not connote any connection with the Hebraic "star of David".

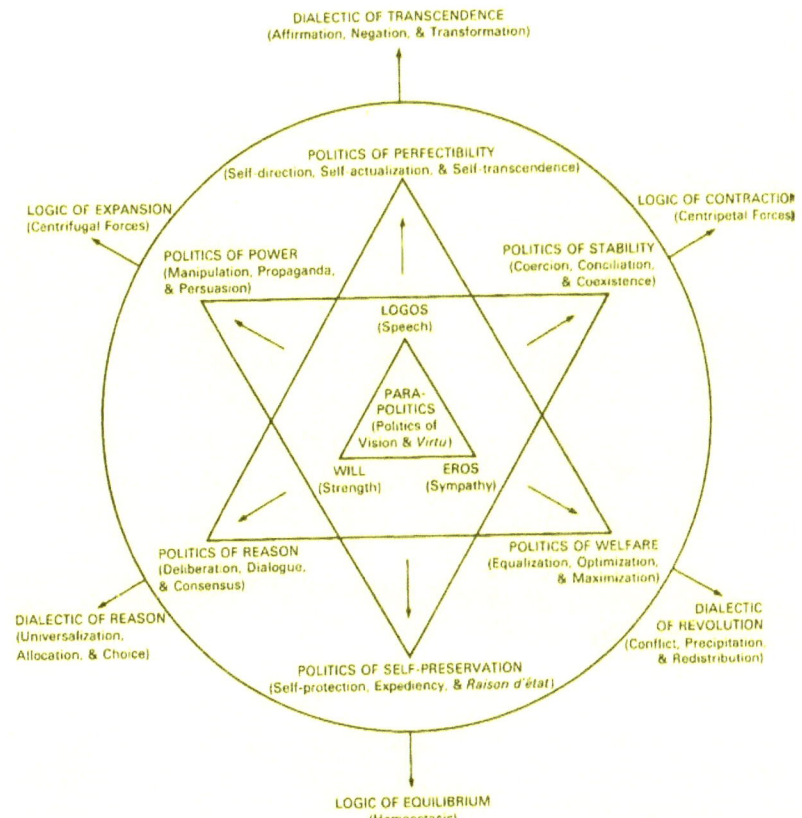

DIALECTIC OF TRANSCENDENCE
(Affirmation, Negation, & Transformation)

POLITICS OF PERFECTIBILITY
(Self-direction, Self-actualization, & Self-transcendence)

LOGIC OF EXPANSION
(Centrifugal Forces)

LOGIC OF CONTRACTION
(Centripetal Forces)

POLITICS OF POWER
(Manipulation, Propaganda,
& Persuasion)

POLITICS OF STABILITY
(Coercion, Conciliation,
& Coexistence)

LOGOS
(Speech)

PARA-
POLITICS
(Politics of
Vision & *Virtu*)

WILL
(Strength)

EROS
(Sympathy)

POLITICS OF REASON
(Deliberation, Dialogue,
& Consensus)

POLITICS OF WELFARE
(Equalization, Optimization,
& Maximization)

DIALECTIC OF REASON
(Universalization,
Allocation, & Choice)

DIALECTIC
OF REVOLUTION
(Conflict, Precipitation,
& Redistribution)

POLITICS OF SELF-PRESERVATION
(Self-protection, Expediency, & *Raison d'état*)

LOGIC OF EQUILIBRIUM
(Homeostasis)

a. 2D>3D>>4D

FindFar is of course a printed book limited to two-dimensional image representations. While in the not-distant future it will doubtless be commonplace for books to conveniently generate 3D holographics when readers turn to those pages, *FindFar* must still tax your imagination for such expansion here.

So this diagram is not really a triangle within a hexagram within a circle. It is a pyramid within a hexagon within a sphere.[65]

The hexagon is omnirotational about the pyramid (which, while 3D, rests stably upon its base as previously described).

The external sphere is similarly omnireferential from the perspectives of the pyramid and hexagon.

Think, therefore, of a three-layered mobile sculpture.

Actually this 3D sculpture is further in 4D motion as discussed in Chapter #2, but one headache at a time.

b. *Agathon* Pyramid: The Core

At the center of the diagram is the *Agathon* Pyramid, resting on its conscious (will) and subconscious (*eros*) bases. Together they energize the *logos*, activating the ParaPolitics manifestations of Platonic vision (*nœsis*) and Machiavellian *virtu*, revealing the governing *Agathon*, whose *neter*/Form then radiates outward throughout all of the diagram's constituent elements.

---

[65] Topologists will be quick to point out that a hexagon has many more than six internal extensions. *Touché*. The point to be taken with this analogy is that the various labelings of the 2D hexagram lines are all equally accessible to/influential upon the entire ParaPolitical dynamic; they are not "hierarchical" or sequential.

c. Types of Politics

ParaPolitics embraces six specialized types or expressions of political thinking, expression, and action, increasing in complexity and nuance as they appear higher on the Pyramid of *Agathon*.

At the base of the Pyramid is the quasi-instinctive Politics of **Self-Preservation**. Here are found all measures sought and taken by a sentient being to protect and continue its existence: the "culture of the caveman", which is "political" only because of the realization of "safety in numbers".

Next higher - that is to say present and emphasized in political entities - are **Power** and **Stability**: the characteristics of a tribe, city-state, or nation-state. Like Self-Preservation, these qualities are generally considered to be essential, not optional.

Neither is inherently altruistic or admirable: Power is exercised by projecting the values of the *polis* beyond its populace and borders through means ranging from propaganda to armed force. Stability of the *polis* is sought by reinforcing education and indoctrination of the citizenry, and if necessary more drastically by repression and punishment.

Next come what amount to options and luxuries: **Reason** and **Welfare**. It is at this level of civilization that, with basic needs of survival ensured, cultures can engage is some flexibility, seeking more satisfaction in various social structures, customs, and conveniences.

A standard of living above that of mere survival also permits luxuries for some or all persons, as well as a measure of provision for those unable to completely take care of themselves.

These categories of politics more-or-less complete what the world regards as the "modern state". It is similarly among these variables that PW cooperation and confrontation occur.

Along the ascent of consciousness, as depicted on the Pyramid, they involve only the lesser-intellectual invocations of *Eikasia* and *Pistis*.

Approaching the apex are the still-rational Politics of **Perfectibility**, characterized by *Dianoia*, and finally the Politics of **Transcendence**, enabled through *Nœsis*. These last two are not employed in PW interactions, but are both essential in MW.

As the hexagram/gon implies, all of these types of politics [except Transcendence] can be mixed and weighted in the design of an ideal *polis*.

In a MW campaign prudently or necessarily limited to an *áristos* resolution, only combinations of the functions of Power, Stability, Reason, and Welfare are developed, with especial consideration given to moderating the first two.

Perfectibility becomes an option in a complete *kalokagathia* design, insofar as it reflects an intentional application of the identified *Agathon*.

d. Internal Stresses & External Pressures

The surrounding circle/sphere illustrates externalities constantly seeking to repress and constrain the *polis*, or to stimulate its propensity and tendency to advertise, export, and expand itself.

Such forces and influences can range from the ideological (the seeking of reassurance and validation from alliances and partners) to debate, tension, or conflict with those who deny such consolation.

The optimal *polis* will aspire to anticipate and manage all such uncertainties with flexibility, tolerance, and empathy.

e. 4D Dynamic

PW-era "regime changes" or "nation building" is habitually a 3D "makeover". Once such changes have been forced into place, their continuation is assumed to be the responsibility of the new governmental structure to sustain itself; if not, PW is reapplied as endlessly as the foreign power deems necessary to its interests and priorities.

MW strategists are not permitted this cavalier sloppiness. Whatever they devise, whether at the levels of *áristos* or *kalokagathia*, must be engineered for operation in a 4D dynamic environment, both internally and externally.

What this means is that the FF projections are continued throughout the *polis*-configuration process, providing the initial design with the flexibility and resources it will need to continue to survive and prosper, harmoniously and rewardingly with its neighbors and partners abroad.

Chapter 5: Complications

[The bankrupt Duchy of Grand Fenwick[66] declared war on the United States in order to lose and be reconstructed. Its boatload of soldiers returns ...]
Grand Duchess Gloriana: How did the war go?
Tully Bascombe: Well, Your Grace, there's been a slight change of plan. We sort of won.
Prime Minister Mountjoy: You sort of **what**?
                                      - *The Mouse That Roared* (1959)

Snakes. Why'd it have to be **snakes**?
                    - Indiana Jones, *Raiders of the Lost Ark* (1981)

A. Snakes!

MindWar is designed to function flawlessly and seamlessly when introduced and activated in a non-destabilized environment.

In such a setting it can establish and maintain, with minimal resources, expense, and effort, a serene and successful outlook as FF-projected and adjusted accordingly by MW TriForce team assets.

In the 21st-Century world as presented by PW, however, MW does not have this luxury. When and where activated, it can expect to arrive in a PW mess approaching meltdown. [Anything short of that will

---

[66] http://ib.frath.net/w/Grand_Fenwick

probably be PW-gnawed until it **is** undeniably a complete failure.]

Additionally in such circumstances MW will probably not have the luxury of a "leisurely calendar". National and regional crises are often rushing towards a mega-crisis, such as an explosion into a much more widespread PW. So MW must not only stabilize the situation, but do so under the pressure of a ticking clock.

What are some of the possible impediments, and how could MW reduce or eliminate them?

B. PW Profitability

1. Extent

As unpalatable as it may be to contemplate, PW stays in business because it **is** business - enormously, extremely profitably so. Indeed it is not hard to argue that "war profiteering" is **the** primary reason for the promulgation and continuation of PWs worldwide, especially by nations (such as the United States, Israel, Russia, China, and much if industrialized Europe) with substantial munitions industries. Just how much does this canary actually weigh?

> U.S. weapons exporters lead the world in profits from the booming military arms and equipment business, driven by rising tensions and conflict around the world, according to a new report from London-based analysts.
> The annual study by IHS Inc. - which looks at military markets in 65 nations, excluding small arms, munitions, and surveillance programs - finds that the United States is behind one-third of all equipment and weapons exports worldwide.
> This is no small amount: In 2014 global "defense" trade surpassed $64.4 billion, the report finds.
> "Defense trade rose by a landmark 13.4 percent over the past year," said Ben Moores, senior defense analyst at IHS Aerospace, Defense and Security, in a press statement. "This

record figure has been driven by unparalleled demand from the emerging economies for military aircraft and an escalation of regional tensions in the Middle East and Asia Pacific."

The U.S. further is the top profiteer from rising conflict across the Middle East, accounting for $8.4 billion in exports to this region in 2014, compared to $6 billion the previous year ...[67]

The United States is by no means the sole addict to this particular economic opiate. The IHS report continues:

> The second tier of exporters to the Middle East is led by the United Kingdom with US$1.9 billion, the Russian Federation with US$1.5 billion, France with US$1.3 billion and Germany with US$1 billion.[68]

MW, by contrast, utilizes **no** PW weaponry at all, either directly used by the United States PW military forces and their covert civilian adjuncts (Central Intelligence Agency, private paramilitary contractors) or indirectly by sales or gifts to PW allies and surrogates.

2. Redirection

Conventional proposals to eliminate war-profiteerism generally default to either socialist nationalization of such industries, eliminating private/corporate/shareholder enrichment, or surrender and subordination of national

---

[67] Lazare, Sarah, "U.S. Weapons Exporters Lead World in War Profiteering", *Common Dreams*, March 9, 2015.
http://www.commondreams.org/news/2015/03/09/us-weapons-exporters-lead-world-war-profiteering

[68] "Saudi Arabia replaces India as largest defence market for US", *IHS Jane's 360*, March 9, 2015.
http://www.janes.com/article/49809/saudi-arabia-replaces-india-as-largest-defence-market-for-us

PW capabilities to a supranational body such as the United Nations. Both options are *prima facie* unrealistic.

The MW solution, which may be considered an admittedly cynical, yet nonetheless effective application of *áristos*, proposes to allow the manufacture, sale, and export of munitions to continue, but to discourage its actual use in favor of mere display and spectacle.

The model for this is the 1947-1991 Cold War between the United States and the Soviet Union. Possession of nuclear arsenals and intercontinental delivery systems more than sufficient to annihilate one another in an [inevitably simultaneous] launch made [hot] PW impossible; the quaint if darkly-apt euphemism was "MAD" (Mutually-Assured Destruction), alternately the "balance of terror".[69]

Instead of the Cold War's eliminating the ostensibly-unusable conventional weapons industries of both superpowers, these paradoxically expanded and also increased production.

Both countries' populations were constantly alarmed by allegations of "missile gaps" [at the time of the Kennedy/Nixon Presidential campaign] or claimed deficiencies in conventional arms so extreme as to possibly embolden the Soviet Union and its Warsaw Pact allies to venture a conventional PW against the United States and NATO, gambling that the conventionally-outmatched West would ultimately not dare the suicidal step of resorting to nuclear weapons, even "battlefield".

This scenario began to gain serious Western credibility during the Carter Administration (1977-80) and was seized upon by the successor Reagan Administration (1981-8) as the centerpiece of its "Evil Empire" propaganda.

---

[69] In the old sense of just being really, **really** scared - not the 21st-Century "Communism!"-replacement monster-under-the-bed of "Terrorism!".

The result was a surge in U.S./NATO conventional armament and deployment which the already-strained Soviet Union found itself economically unable to match, even with maximum extractions from its Warsaw Pact satellites. Hence the collapse of the Eastern economy and Western Cold War "victory" at the end of that decade.

An interesting "sideshow" of this sinister circus was the United States' invention of the "neutron bomb" in 1977. More precisely titled the "Enhanced Radiation Warhead" (ERW), this was a nuclear weapon which emitted a life- but not property-destroying burst of neutron radiation. The idea was that, fitted to battlefield-level missiles such as the Corporal and Sergeant, it could stop a Warsaw Pact armored offensive [literally] "dead in its tracks" without contaminating any territory or destroying any structures.

Suddenly it appeared that the "nuclear threshold" could be crossed tactically without triggering an "ordinary" thermonuclear holocaust.

The East was obviously not pleased at this prospect, and argued furiously against it both diplomatically and publicly.

President Carter finally decided that the ERW would be produced and deployed only if at least two other NATO member-nations would agree to host such missiles. West Germany agreed if a second could be found. Turkey secretly became that second, but Carter chose not to publicize this and ERW faded away as a Cold War crisis.[70]

Meanwhile the brandishing of weaponry was a testosteronic regularity, from May Day parades in Moscow to ceaseless "war games" in Western Europe. At sea both blocs showed off their latest nuclear submarines

---

[70] The complete story of this curious episode may be studied in the author's book *The Neutron Bomb*. San Francisco: Barony of Rachane, 2016.

and hi-tech surface ships, while ever-more-advanced aircraft and military-satellite launches culminated in extraordinarily-expensive missile-defense concepts [such as the United States' "Safeguard"] and President Reagan's LucasFilm-inspired "Star Wars" satellite-warfare technology.

Not to stray from the point here, many of these exoticities were never deployed or even built beyond the experimental stage, but as far as they went, they cost taxpayers substantial amounts of money, which lined the pockets of military, naval, and ærospace contractors.

The intercontinental ballistic missile standoff between the United States and post-USSR Russian Federation remains as formidable as ever during the Cold War, opening the door to a "Cold War II" with renewed munitions-profiteer windfalls.

This is hardly an ideal *áristos*, since the original peril of an accidental ICBM-triggering remains. That said, this peril has never disappeared, even after the end of Cold War I.

The present orgy of sales and use of conventional arms throughout the Middle East could be curtailed in favor of Cold War II *braggadocio*: the continued flow of money without the flow of blood.

If there is a downside to this caustically bottom-feeding *áristos*, it is that with full strategic attention once again fixated on a renewed "balance of terror", there is theoretically that much more chance of a fatally "nervous mistake", such as the 1962 "Cuban Missile Crisis" came perilously close to being.

Cold War II, if inaugurated, must take care to indulge flamboyant posturing and pretentiousness - but nowhere near the push-button.

C. Politics of Stability

1. "War is Peace"

In addition to a PW-*habitué* nation's financial-profiteering motives, an ongoing PW serves to increase public docility and obedience by emotionally uniting the masses against a proclaimed foreign enemy threat. Beyond this it inspires voluntary work and sacrifice as an expression and passionate release of "patriotism". In *1984* George Orwell glacially but definitively summarized this rationale thus:

> War, it will be seen, accomplishes the necessary destruction, but accomplishes it in a psychologically acceptable way. In principle it would be quite simple to waste the surplus labour of the world by building temples and pyramids, by digging holes and filling them up again, or even by producing vast quantities of goods and then setting fire to them. But this would provide only the economic and not the emotional basis for a hierarchical society. What is concerned here is not the morale of masses, whose attitude is unimportant so long as they are kept steadily at work, but the morale of the Party itself. Even the humblest Party member is expected to be competent, industrious, and even intelligent within narrow limits, but it is also necessary that he should be a credulous and ignorant fanatic whose prevailing moods are fear, hatred, adulation, and orgiastic triumph. In other words it is necessary that he should have the mentality appropriate to a state of war. It does not matter whether the war is actually happening, and, since no decisive victory is possible, it does not matter whether the war is going well or badly. All that is needed is that a state of war should exist.[71]

In the Pyramid of *Agathon* and ParaPolitics schematics, this appears as the "Politics of Stability", the inward-coercive counterforce to the outward-aggressive

---

[71] "War is Peace", *1984*, *op. cit.*, 1949, page #158.

"Politics of Power". Together they serve as the state's ultimate binding mechanism.

In Oliver Stone's reflection upon the assassination of President John Kennedy, a retired "Black Ops" officer observes indifferently to the New Orleans District Attorney:

> The organizing principle of any society, Mr. Garrison, is for war. The authority of the state over its people resides in its war powers.
> Kennedy wanted to end the Cold War in his second term.
> He wanted to call off the Moon race and cooperate with the Soviets.
> He signed a treaty to ban nuclear testing.
> He refused to invade Cuba in 1962.
> He set out to withdraw from Vietnam.
> But all that ended on the 22nd of November, 1963.[72]

2. Rehab

As with PW-profiteering, PW-passion is so deeply integrated into and characteristic of the contemporary nation-state that it cannot be directly removed.

Indeed any obvious effort to do so would be interpreted by the state as a dangerous threat tantamount

---

[72] The unidentified officer "X" in Stone's *JFK* was in fact Colonel L. Fletcher Prouty (USAF-Ret.), a close friend of the author who had served as Chief of Special Operations for the Joint Chiefs of Staff during the Kennedy Administration. In a July 2, 1995 letter to the author, Prouty identified his immediate superior, Major General Edward Lansdale, as the architect and executor of the assassination: "He had hundreds of trained and skilled men [from Operation MONGOOSE] whom he could use to flesh out the cover story that the true decision-makers had to have to protect the real hit team, and create the three decades of cover story that has embarrassed American citizens since that date. Without such a cover story the murder and resultant *coup d'etat* could not have been achieved so effectively. JFK would not give him that [South Vietnam] Ambassadorship for which he would have killed. What else could he do?"

to treason, provoking a response similar to that visited upon J.F.K.

Instead MW must seek not to "cold turkey" national PW-addiction, but rather to shift it to a less-murderous fixation.

Some smaller nations, fortunate not to be burdened with superpower-political self-images, indeed have successfully crafted a *raison d'état* for themselves on some other basis.

Switzerland justifies itself as a bastion of international financial security, and also as sponsor of independent humanitarian activities such as the Red Cross.

Various Scandinavian countries have sought to be havens for other nations' political refugees.

Even some historic lands such as Egypt and Greece, despite too-close-for-comfort PW-surrounds, prefer to market themselves as tourist attractions.

In the case of the PW-hooked superpowers, such a cure is not as unrealistic or elusive as it might seem at first glance.

The exemplar here happens to be China, perhaps surprisingly given its Cold War *persona* as a Maoist monastery more doctrinaire than even its Stalinist model across the Great Wall. Today it shows little interest in any PW-projection beyond what it regards as its millennia-old turf, preferring adventures in finance, technology, manufacturing [including for export], and cultural *chic*.

The U.S. Obama Administration, casting about for a scarecrow to replace the by-now-motheaten "Terrorism!", attempted to promote a sort of "neo-China-containment" Pacific Rim militarization, unfortunately regarded by both China and America as comically-boring: Even a cold war requires the other party to be interested, and China's actual interest in the United States is more towards investment and real estate ownership.

In annoyance Obama turned back to Russia, hoping that the latter's activities in the Crimea and Ukraine might be an excuse for neo-NATOism. Once again Russia doesn't seem to be particularly interested, with Vladimir Putin declining to don Darth Vader's costume for a lightsaber duel with either Luke Obama or Yoda Trump.

So, since as of early 2017 both Eastasia and Eurasia aren't being PW-cooperative, the United States is reduced to still trying to pump more air into the disintegrating tire of "Terrorism!".

Certainly decades of Middle East economic strangulation, bombing, invasion, and occupation have generated more than a few vengeful expatiates, but somehow it just isn't as nightmarifying as the old E-ticket ride of imminent nuclear annihilation.

So in the case of the United States, this melodrama has yet to play out - perhaps, if all monster-hunts fail, towards a merchandising alternative as salutary as our own tourism. There is, after all, plenty to see and enjoy throughout all fifty states and the Beltway cage. We really don't need to keep tying up Sweet Sue:

> Salty Sam was tryin' to stuff Sweet Sue in a burlap sack, he said
> "If you don't give me the deed to your ranch, I'm gonna throw you
>   on the railroad tracks!"
> And then he grabbed her (and **then**?)
> He tied her up (and **then**?)
> He threw her on the railroad tracks (and **then**?)
> A train started comin' (and **then**, and **THEN**?)
> - And then along came Jones:
> Tall, thin Jones,
> Slow-walkin' Jones,
> Slow-talkin' Jones,
> Along came long, lean, lanky Jones.[73]

---

[73] The Coasters, "Along Came Jones", 1959.

D. Revolution

1. A Party in Progress

When one nation decides to PW-insert itself into the affairs of another, the general assumption is that there will be a government presently in place to be subjugated or replaced with fresh puppetry.

However some situations of instability may not involve only actions between predefined national actors, but may extend to structural breakdown within one or more of the object nations: factional infighting or more comprehensive nationwide revolutionary efforts.

On the ParaPolitics diagram this is recognized as the centrifugal "Dialectic of Revolution". It is massively destabilizing, often to the point of rendering any outside intervention impotent, or at best of peripheral influence. One need only look back to the major such revolutions of history - the American, French, English, and Russian to cite the most famous - and of course to innumerable less well-known examples.

By their very nature, moreover, revolutions are non-standardized:

- They may be more or less bloodless, or quite the other extreme.

- They may be widespread mobilizations or close-held *coups d'état*.

- They may or may not be ideology- or religion-based.

- They may be over in hours or drag on for years.

- They may be purely the instigation of the national populace, or the surrogates of foreign antagonists.

And frequently various combinations of the above.

PW intervention in such situations is typically unable to offer anything but an even more brutal combative presence, the presumption being to suppress the existing infighting by sheer weight of superior force. The

American Revolution saw attempted intervention by both Britain and France, and the Russian Revolution by a number of capitalist and monarchist nations unified in their fear of the communist "germ". At this writing Syria continues to be torn apart by internal factions, regional movements, and external national entities such as Russia, America, Iran, and Turkey.

Even should a given revolution be successful, as in the example of the creation of the Islamic State from conquered portions of Syria and Iraq, there remains the question of internationally-recognized legitimacy.

Again history provides many instances of relatively quick recognition [as in the case of the United States] as well as reluctant, grudging acceptance [as with the Soviet Union and the People's Republic of China]. Sometimes it is only the appearance of a perceived greater threat, such as Nazi Germany in the 1930s, that brings "strange bedfellows" at least temporarily together in formal recognition presaging alliance: The once-pernicious Stalin suddenly became affable "Uncle Joe".

2. Crashing the Party

a. *Status Quo Ante*

When faced with a revolutionary situation, MW's first recourse is a detailed investigation into the **causes** which gave rise to it - not the dramatics of the present symptoms.

This is in effect 4D FF "in reverse", going back through time in search of a previous stability if any.

The logical consequence of this is to ascertain whether it is in any way possible to "roll back" the present to the previous - and if not, why not.

In such an analysis the overall present is also broken down into as many parts as may be material and identifiable.

b. Retubing Toothpaste?

Establishing a clear and accurate picture of the *status quo ante* is one thing; returning a current destabilization to it is quite another.

What may seem to some - especially those most favored of it - as a "golden age" is rather unlikely to be that for the revolutionaries. In all likelihood the irritants that inspired the revolution were already there, just suppressed and not yet raised to the boiling-point.

Hence MW is not so naïve as to attempt a return to the past. What the FD establishes is an understanding of the revolutionary forces at work, not an *áristos*, much less *kalokagathia*. One or the other of these prescriptions will require FF and the *Agathon*/ParaPolitics exercises described in the preceding chapter.

c. Conflicted Drives

Once social forces have become strong enough to spark a revolution, the fixation of the revolutionaries is directly and immediately the catalyst of its success. While there may be moral and ideological values at play, such as redistribution of land-ownership or the institution of a preferred theocracy, these remain to be argued-out once the old order is eliminated.

A true revolution is not a statement of reform or replacement of existing institutions or officialdom. It is an enraged statement of total annihilation of the existing order, on the presumption that it is utterly beyond reform or redemption; nothing of it must survive.

It is thus that revolutions generate a kinetic passion which, while extent, is nigh unstoppable: a runaway train.

MW has little alternative but to wait until this frenzy has run its course, by either success or failure.

The following example, fully half a century prior to the Russian Revolution, serves as a chilling illustration of these cataclysms:

d. Dæmonic Possession

The embrace of revolutionary fervor to the utter eclipse of every other emotion or value was seen and enunciated most incisively in the anarchistic-conspiracy preludes to the 1917 Russian Revolution, by an obsessed visionary, Sergey Genadievich Nechayev. Unsurprisingly his was an unwelcome voice in Czarist Russia, and he died in prison in 1882 at the young age of 35 - but not before he had penned his *Revolutionary Catechism* in 1869.[74] This remarkable document bears careful attention of all who would seek to either initiate or forestall political revolutions:

The Revolutionary Catechism

Duties of the Revolutionary toward Himself

1. The revolutionary is a doomed man. He has no personal interests, no business affairs, no emotions, no attachments, no property, and no name. Everything in him is wholly absorbed in the single thought and the single passion for revolution.

2. The revolutionary knows that in the very depths of his being, not only in words but also in deeds, he has broken all the bonds which tie him to the social order and the civilized world with all its laws, moralities, and customs,

---

[74] Already a legend during his short lifetime, Nechayev was portrayed in Fyodor Dostoyevsky's 1872 novel *Dæmons* (also known as *The Possessed*).

and with all its generally accepted conventions. He is their implacable enemy, and if he continues to live with them it is only in order to destroy them more speedily.

3. The revolutionary despises all doctrines and refuses to accept the mundane sciences, leaving them for future generations. He knows only one science: the science of destruction. For this reason, but only for this reason, he will study mechanics, physics, chemistry, and perhaps medicine. But all day and all night he studies the vital science of human beings, their characteristics and circumstances, and all the phenomena of the present social order. The object is perpetually the same: the surest and quickest way of destroying the whole filthy order.

4. The revolutionary despises public opinion. He despises and hates the existing social morality in all its manifestations. For him, morality is everything which contributes to the triumph of the revolution. Immoral and criminal is everything that stands in its way.

5. The revolutionary is a dedicated man, merciless toward the State and toward the educated classes; and he can expect no mercy from them. Between him and them there exists, declared or concealed, a relentless and irreconcilable war to the death. He must accustom himself to torture.

6. Tyrannical toward himself, he must be tyrannical toward others. All the gentle and enervating sentiments of kinship, love, friendship, gratitude, and even honor, must be suppressed in him and give place to the cold and single-minded passion for revolution. For him, there exists only one pleasure, on consolation, one reward, one satisfaction — the success of the revolution. Night and day he must have but one thought, one aim — merciless destruction. Striving cold-bloodedly and indefatigably toward this end, he must be prepared to destroy himself and to destroy with his own hands everything that stands in the path of the revolution.

7. The nature of the true revolutionary excludes all sentimentality, romanticism, infatuation, and exaltation. All private hatred and revenge must also be excluded. Revolutionary passion, practiced at every moment of the

day until it becomes a habit, is to be employed with cold calculation. At all times, and in all places, the revolutionary must obey not his personal impulses, but only those which serve the cause of the revolution.

Relations of the Revolutionary toward his Comrades

8. The revolutionary can have no friendship or attachment, except for those who have proved by their actions that they, like him, are dedicated to revolution. The degree of friendship, devotion and obligation toward such a comrade is determined solely by the degree of his usefulness to the cause of total revolutionary destruction.

9. It is superfluous to speak of solidarity among revolutionaries. The whole strength of revolutionary work lies in this. Comrades who possess the same revolutionary passion and understanding should, as much as possible, deliberate all important matters together and come to unanimous conclusions. When the plan is finally decided upon, then the revolutionary must rely solely on himself. In carrying out acts of destruction, each one should act alone, never running to another for advice and assistance, except when these are necessary for the furtherance of the plan.

10. All revolutionaries should have under them second- or third-degree revolutionaries – i.e., comrades who are not completely initiated. these should be regarded as part of the common revolutionary capital placed at his disposal. This capital should, of course, be spent as economically as possible in order to derive from it the greatest possible profit. The real revolutionary should regard himself as capital consecrated to the triumph of the revolution; however, he may not personally and alone dispose of that capital without the unanimous consent of the fully initiated comrades.

11. When a comrade is in danger and the question arises whether he should be saved or not saved, the decision must not be arrived at on the basis of sentiment, but solely in the interests of the revolutionary cause. Therefore, it is necessary to weigh carefully the usefulness of the comrade against the expenditure of

revolutionary forces necessary to save him, and the decision must be made accordingly.

Relations of the Revolutionary toward Society

12. The new member, having given proof of his loyalty not by words but by deeds, can be received into the society only by the unanimous agreement of all the members.

13. The revolutionary enters the world of the State, of the privileged classes, of the so-called civilization, and he lives in this world only for the purpose of bringing about its speedy and total destruction. He is not a revolutionary if he has any sympathy for this world. He should not hesitate to destroy any position, any place, or any man in this world. He must hate everyone and everything in it with an equal hatred. All the worse for him if he has any relations with parents, friends, or lovers; he is no longer a revolutionary if he is swayed by these relationships.

14. Aiming at implacable revolution, the revolutionary may and frequently must live within society will pretending to be completely different from what he really is, for he must penetrate everywhere, into all the higher and middle-classes, into the houses of commerce, the churches, and the palaces of the aristocracy, and into the worlds of the bureaucracy and literature and the military, and also into the Third Division and the Winter Palace of the Czar.

15. This filthy social order can be split up into several categories. The first category comprises those who must be condemned to death without delay. Comrades should compile a list of those to be condemned according to the relative gravity of their crimes; and the executions should be carried out according to the prepared order.

16. When a list of those who are condemned is made, and the order of execution is prepared, no private sense of outrage should be considered, nor is it necessary to pay attention to the hatred provoked by these people among the comrades or the people. Hatred and the sense of outrage may even be useful insofar as they incite the masses to revolt. It is necessary to be guided only by the relative usefulness of these executions for the sake of

revolution. Above all, those who are especially inimical to the revolutionary organization must be destroyed; their violent and sudden deaths will produce the utmost panic in the government, depriving it of its will to action by removing the cleverest and most energetic supporters.

17. The second group comprises those who will be spared for the time being in order that, by a series of monstrous acts, they may drive the people into inevitable revolt.

18. The third category consists of a great many brutes in high positions, distinguished neither by their cleverness nor their energy, while enjoying riches, influence, power, and high positions by virtue of their rank. These must be exploited in every possible way; they must be implicated and embroiled in our affairs, their dirty secrets must be ferreted out, and they must be transformed into slaves. Their power, influence, and connections, their wealth and their energy, will form an inexhaustible treasure and a precious help in all our undertakings.

19. The fourth category comprises ambitious office-holders and liberals of various shades of opinion. The revolutionary must pretend to collaborate with them, blindly following them, while at the same time, prying out their secrets until they are completely in his power. They must be so compromised that there is no way out for them, and then they can be used to create disorder in the State.

20. The fifth category consists of those doctrinaires, conspirators, and revolutionists who cut a great figure on paper or in their cliques. They must be constantly driven on to make compromising declarations: as a result, the majority of them will be destroyed, while a minority will become genuine revolutionaries.

21. The sixth category is especially important: women. They can be divided into three main groups. First, those frivolous, thoughtless, and vapid women, whom we shall use as we use the third and fourth category of men. Second, women who are ardent, capable, and devoted, but whom do not belong to us because they have not yet achieved a passionless and austere revolutionary understanding; these must be used like the men of the fifth category. Finally, there are the women who are

completely on our side – i.e., those who are wholly dedicated and who have accepted our program in its entirety. We should regard these women as the most valuable or our treasures; without their help, we would never succeed.

Attitude of the Society toward the People

22. The Society has no aim other than the complete liberation and happiness of the masses – i.e., of the people who live by manual labor. Convinced that their emancipation and the achievement of this happiness can only come about as a result of an all-destroying popular revolt, the Society will use all its resources and energy toward increasing and intensifying the evils and miseries of the people until at last their patience is exhausted and they are driven to a general uprising.

23. By a revolution, the Society does not mean an orderly revolt according to the classic western model – a revolt which always stops short of attacking the rights of property and the traditional social systems of so-called civilization and morality. Until now, such a revolution has always limited itself to the overthrow of one political form in order to replace it by another, thereby attempting to bring about a so-called revolutionary state. The only form of revolution beneficial to the people is one which destroys the entire State to the roots and exterminated all the state traditions, institutions, and classes in Russia.

24. With this end in view, the Society therefore refuses to impose any new organization from above. Any future organization will doubtless work its way through the movement and life of the people; but this is a matter for future generations to decide. Our task is terrible, total, universal, and merciless destruction.

25. Therefore, in drawing closer to the people, we must above all make common cause with those elements of the masses which, since the foundation of the state of Muscovy, have never ceased to protest, not only in words but in deeds, against everything directly or indirectly connected with the state: against the nobility, the bureaucracy, the clergy, the traders, and the parasitic kulaks. We must unite with the adventurous tribes of

brigands, who are the only genuine revolutionaries in Russia.

26. To weld the people into one single unconquerable and all-destructive force – this is our aim, our conspiracy, and our task.

e. *Occasione*

In the very apocalypse of revolution lies its redemption. In the wake of its triumph it leaves both a complete political vacuum and the absence of an agenda to fill it.

The Russian Revolution was neither begun nor accomplished by the Communists; Lenin emerged as the enduring successor only after an *interregnum* of confusion and indecision: Kerensky's futile ballet of nostalgic constitutionalism.

The French Revolution was followed by the Terror, ironically subsiding with the ascendancy of an emperor, Napoleon Bonaparte, in place of the beheaded King Louis XVI.

The fledgling United States fared little better: Years of argument following the victory over the British at Yorktown produced in 1781 the Articles of Confederation and Perpetual Union, which "perpetuity" managed less than a decade before replacement by the Constitution. Even then, in another sixty years, the "more perfect union" was ripped asunder by the Civil War.

The message for MW is clear: The immediate post-revolutionary vacuum is Machiavelli's *occasione*: the ideal opportunity for the presentation, acceptance, and promulgation of a previously and carefully devised *kalokagathia*, or at least *áristos* to replace chaos with *civitas*.

E. Identity & Legitimacy

1. "Denn die Todten Reiten Schnell"[75]

Presumably in some blissfully-remote *Shangri-la* of cartographic lamas, the nations of Planet Earth are as defined and pedigreed as they appear on a painted globe. Down in the Valley of the Shadow of Death, however, this is scarcely the case. National borders change through wars or factional *fiat* [as with Russia's 2014 re-acquisition of the Crimea].

Artificial countries are established by departing colonial masters, as with India and Pakistan by Britain.

International collaboration may recognize, if not authorize entirely new countries out of someone else's property, as the United Nations did regarding the Jewish-proclaimed Israel in 1948.

"National" boundaries frequently clash with tribal, ethnic, and/or religious groupings, as in the post-World War I British & French chopfest of the defeated/collapsed Ottoman Empire into the wholly-artificial new states of Turkey, Syria, Mesopotamia (Iraq), Lebanon, and Palestine.

After World War II the United Nations outlawed appropriating populations' sovereign property, except of course where it did so itself, as in the aforementioned recognition of Israel.

In the centuries prior to this convention, to be sure, nations stole from one another all the time, including territory which arguably didn't pre-belong to either party.

Thus it was inconceivable that the Western Hemisphere should be considered the legitimate property of heathen savages such as the Inca, Toltecs, Aztecs, and

---

[75] "... for the dead travel fast." from the 1773 ballad *Lenore* by Gottfried August Bürger, famously quoted by Bram Stoker in his 1897 novel *Dracula*.

numerous northern native tribes. Such inconveniences were mostly dealt with by complete genocide, with concentration camps (called "reservations") for the few survivors.

In the enlightened civilization of modernity, these old faded and forgotten horrors are at least somewhat ritualistically acknowledged and shamed, but never quite to the point of actually returning any of the loot.

2. Dilemma

The author, and perhaps the reader as well, is tempted to see in MindWar an extraordinarily altruistic and humanitarian mechanism. And so it indeed aspires to be.

Nevertheless it must never be forgotten that it is new medicine applied to injuries to which humanity has long since become resigned, if not enthused.

The true MWarrior must therefore pursue his craft conscientiously while at the same time appreciating its limitations. There is much that MW can cure; there is a great deal more that it cannot.

Where the identity and legitimacy of specified MW subjects are concerned, this mechanism confronts its ultimate conditional. The formulation of an *áristos* or *kalokagathia* has everything to do with the application of an appropriate, defining, and fulfilling collective morality: the *Agathon*. This absolutely prerequires an established, immutable identity: a stable platform upon which to raise the temple: an Acropolis for the Parthenon.

During the diagnostic sequence leading to the campaign-operational Foundation Diagnosis (FD), therefore, due attention must be paid to stresses and imbalances behind and beneath the currently-apparent ones. It is folly to "fix" a "nation" whose people may consider it nothing of the sort at all, hence would take little interest in seeing it polished and prosperous.

Accordingly it is entirely possible that a thorough FD may ultimately yield the disconcerting prospectus that, as predefined, there is in finality **no** nation to rescue.

What may be called for is more invasive surgery: the complete redrawing of borders, reidentification of constituencies, perhaps to the nascent glory of a new name.

In the Middle East of the early 21st Century, two cases-in-point are notably conspicuous: the Kurds and the Islamic State.

Ethnic Kurds inhabit a contiguous area, unofficially "Kurdistan", including portions of Turkey, Syria, and Iraq. To the present this has not asserted itself into implacable revolutionary zeal [see above *Catechism*], though there is constant and varying tension as one or more of the "legitimate" nations may attempt to reinforce claims of sovereignty.

The flipside of this is that any attempts to improve the national profiles of those same three claimants while ignoring "Kurdistan" would be, in a word, fatuous.

At least the Kurds enjoy a general, if awkward, favor in the eyes of the established international community. Not so the Islamic State, an entity which materialized from the post-American-occupation ruin of Iraq.

Prior to the 2003 American invasion, Saddam Hussein's regime had been a stable, if authoritarian mix of [minority] Sunni and [majority] Shiite Muslims. Since the Sunnis held the reins of governmental power, Iraq served among other things as a regional counterweight to Shiite Iran, indeed to the extent of an exhaustive if inconclusive war between the two nations 1980-88.

In "regime-changing" Iraq following its invasion of that country, the United States effectively swept aside the Sunnis, leaving no residual alternative but to concoct a replacement from the Shiites. The we-should-have-seen-this-coming result was an Iraqi government significantly under the influence, if not outright control of Iran (a nation not exactly on America's Christmas-card list ever since it kicked out the CIA-anointed Shah back in 1979).

In Baghdad the newly-empowered Shiites, who had previously suffered oppression, imprisonment, and occasional execution by the Hussein-regime Sunnis, duly devoted the next decade to returning the disfavor.

The cumulative consequence was an uprising by various enclaves of Sunnis, which finally came together as a new nation, announcing itself the Islamic State (IS).[76]

IS promptly proceeded to assert the normal, time-honored prerogatives of a sovereign nation by defending its borders and imprisoning or killing foreign attackers and its own disobedient citizens.

The problem was that these are the prerogatives of only "legitimate" nations, more-or-less equating to United Nations recognition, and to date IS has not been granted this birth certificate.

As accordingly an "international bastard" IS' exercise of the aforementioned violence is thus not a right but an outrage, justifying righteous calls by the outraged for its extermination. IS, territorially vulnerable to the massed might of superpowers, has unsurprisingly responded by progressively becoming less "territorial", morphing into a mobile-cellular international attack conglomerate very much like its similarly non-territorial predecessor *al-Qaida*. So its would-be exterminators have traded a single, tangible target for an unknown, scattered number of intangible ones: yet another PW strategy leaving something to be desired.

---

[76] As IS asserted sovereignty over a portion of Syria as well, it became colloquially the "Islamic State of Iraq and Syria", or "ISIS" - arousing at least the author's indignation on behalf of the ancient Egyptian *neter* Isis, whose ineffable name is thus, if only coincidentally, blasphemed.

From a MW perspective, this existing PW response to IS is virtually predesigned to fail. IS is the "rope" in a multidirectional tug-of-war involving Turkey, Syria, Baghdad-Iraq, Iran, the United States, Saudi Arabia, Israel, and Russia [at minimum]. There is obviously nothing remotely close to a consensus among all these tuggers - and meanwhile strands of the rope continue to proliferate elsewhere around the world.

Were this situation handed over to the MW TriForce, its solution might proceed something like this:

1. Immediately remove all PW forces from the original IS territory.

2. For the duration of the MW campaign, blanket the entire IS, as well as the Syrian and Baghdad capitals, with PSYCONs to minimize antagonism and maximize creative cooperation.

3. Have MFB establish an on-site presence in the IS capital, and open immediate contact with its government.

4. Emplace MFB teams with the Syrian and Baghdad governments.

5. Through the three MFB teams, arrange for Syria and Baghdad to cede their IS-occupied territory to that state in return for its further non-expansion.

6. Assign PPB teams to accomplish IS' international recognition, e.g. the United Nations.

Áristos is now tentatively established, but the three MFB teams remain in place, and the MWB PSYCON blanket continues, until stability appears normalized. At that point MFB is withdrawn and replaced by PPB in IS only, to guide its peaceful and constructive development as a new nation. The MWB PSYCON blanket is withdrawn from Syria and Baghdad, but remains in place over IS until PPB deems it no longer necessary.

Now assured of its safety from invasion, IS ceases all of its worldwide paramilitary operations as a condition of its recognized legitimacy. It provides both Syria and Baghdad with open access to their former territories, to facilitate impacted residents' comfort and consideration.

This entire MW campaign, if given full international cooperation and non-interference, should be complete within a year of Declaration.

F. *Metropolis*

1. **Technostate**

In 1960s' Political Science circles there was increasing speculation, indeed anticipation of an impending eclipse of the centuries-familiar nation/state frame of reference by a new monster called the "multinational corporation". The largest business ventures had begun to establish their footing in several industrialized countries around the globe, as well as resource-extraction operations throughout the "third world" of the pre-industrialized. The fear was that such multilocated entities would forego allegiance to any one parent-state, choosing rather to support the most profitable side of any international dispute.

As the decades rolled onward, this spectre indeed materialized, but along with it came a derivative arguably even more sinister: the transformation of human values into technological ones.

Traditionally the biological human being has been the substance of society, whether individually *or en masse*. But along with the proliferation of computers, "smart phones", and other population-pervasive cybernetics came the gradual revaluation of humans not as users of, but as used by these appendages.

The conquest of organic life by inorganic machines has long been a staple of science-fiction, from the benevolent babysitters of Isaac Asimov's *I, Robot* and Jack Williamson's *The Humanoids* to not-so-benevolent extraterrestrials: *Battlestar Galactica*'s Cylons, *Star Trek*'s Borg, and *Stargate*'s Replicators. But what parents and educators are suddenly worrying about is something much more subtle, and unnervingly science-**fact**: that iPhone-suckled generations are growing up conditioned to process thoughts more like the machines who are increasingly their **actual** babysitters, friends, and teachers.

This transition from organic-analogic to inorganic-digitalogic sacrifices intangibles and abstractions for the speed and precision of either/or simplification.

Along the way the metaphysical, divine soul of the individual human being is first ignored, then discarded, and finally intentionally destroyed as an irrelevant obsolescence.[77]

Even the most venerable universities, besieged by a generation of students desperate for a foothold in the increasingly competitive and shrinking technological job market, are neglecting the Humanities (!) in favor of career-practical curricula.

---

[77] To more thoroughly appreciate the danger of such metaphysical suicide, see the author's *MindStar* (2016).

In this de-intellectualization environment, as elsewhere, George Orwell foresaw humanity's regression towards the complete atrophy of consciousness:

> By 2050 - earlier, probably - all real knowledge of Oldspeak will have disappeared. The whole literature of the past will have been destroyed. Chaucer, Shakespeare, Milton, Byron - they'll exist only in Newspeak versions, not merely changed into something different, but actually changed into something contradictory of what they used to be. Even the literature of the Party will change. Even the slogans will change. How could you have a slogan like "Freedom is Slavery" when the concept of freedom has been abolished? The whole climate of thought will be different. In fact there will **be** no thought as we understand it now. Orthodoxy means not thinking - not needing to think. Orthodoxy is unconsciousness.[78]

At the beginning of the 20th Century, in Expressionist Germany, Thea von Harbou envisioned just such a future in her novel *Metropolis*, in which only a rarified elite (very much like today's notorious "1%") enjoy sybaritic leisure while, in hideous subterranean factories, the masses of humanity toil endlessly, mindlessly as slaves of behemoth machines.[79]

2. *Ultima Futura*

The dismal horror of *Metropolis* was redeemed by revolution, but not as Nechayev would have recognized it. It was not an apocalypse of violence, but a reconciliation, or as von Harbou phrased it, "mediation of head and hands by the heart".

Catalyst of this salvation was a beatific woman, Maria - but not before she was kidnapped and duplicated as an

---

[78] Syme to Winston Smith in *1984, op. cit.*, page #47.

[79] In 1927 *Metropolis* was made into the classic motion picture by Thea's husband Fritz Lang.

evil robotrix, the [in]famous *Ultima Futura*, who very nearly orchestrated the destruction of the entire *polis* in a nihilistic *bacchanale* of orgiastic savagery.

In this prescient parable may perhaps be glimpsed the MW solution to onrushing technocracy: not insertion of an even more potent "robotrix" of MWB PSYCONs, but the PPB invocation of the original, innocent "spirit of humanity" - our own "Maria" - to remind and restore both "heads" and "hands" of a technostate to the primal innocence of a shared "heart".

This is perhaps the most elusive of MW avenues to identify and navigate, but the impulse to find it - the mythic Grail Quest - is as old as humanity itself. In any case there may be no alternative.

G. "Learn to Smile"

This has been a sobering, indeed chilling chapter to write, and doubtless to read - speaking as it does to the *menagerie* of monsters under MW's bed: complications and consternations which can confound otherwise-impeccable MW evaluations, campaigns, and perfections. MW, as refined an art and science as it is, is nonetheless subject to the *schadenfroh* curse of Murphy's Law.

The lesson in this for the aspiring MWarrior is to always temper idealism with pragmatism: to anticipate a menu of more *áristos* than *kalokagathia*, and even then to be prepared for an *áristos* that may only barely suffice. What **is** important is to seek and realize it nevertheless.

In John Fowles' *The Magus*, protagonist Nicholas Urfe despairs of the rampant hypocrisy he sees about him in the Postmodern world, and very nearly surrenders to it in a battle for his own soul between the "Maria" of his true love Alison and the "robotrix" of the seductive siren Lily.

Overseeing Nicholas' "election" - the sheer hazard of being forced to choose - is the "magus" Maurice Conchis ...

> A figure appeared in the door. It was Conchis. He came and stood in front of me.
> "I come to tell you that you are now elect."
> I shook my head violently from side to side.
> "You have no choice."
> I still shook my head, but more wearily.
> He stared at me, with those eyes that seemed older than one man's lifetime, and a little gleam of sympathy came into his expression, as if after all he might have put too much pressure on a very thin lever.
> "Learn to smile, Nicholas. Learn to smile."
> It came to me then that he meant something different by "smile": that the irony, the humorlessness, the ruthlessness I had always noted in his smiling was a quality he deliberately inserted; that for him the smile was something essentially cruel, because freedom is cruel, because the freedom that makes us at least partly responsible for what we are is cruel. Hence for him the smile was not so much an **attitude** to be taken to life as rather the **nature** of the cruelty of life, a cruelty we cannot even choose to avoid, since it is inherent in human existence.
> He meant something far stranger by "learn to smile" than the banal "grin and bear it". If anything it meant "learn to be cruel; learn to be dry; learn to survive".
> That we have no choice of play or role. It is always *Othello*. To be is, inexorably, to be Iago.
> He gave me the smallest of bows, one full of irony, of the contempt implicit in incongruous courtesy, then went.[80]

As now this book.

---

[80] [Abridged from] Fowles, John, *The Magus* (revised edition). Boston: Little, Brown & Company, 1977, page #531.

Afterword

The Prince and the Magician[81]

Once upon a time there was a young prince, who believed in all things but three. He did not believe in princesses, he did not believe in islands, he did not believe in God. His father, the king, told him that such things did not exist. As there were no princesses or islands in his father's domaines, and no sign of God, the young prince believed his father.

But then, one day, the prince ran away from his palace. He came to the next land. There, to his astonishment, from every coast he saw islands, and on these islands, strange and troubling creatures whom he dared not name. As he was searching for a boat, a man in full evening dress approached him along the shore.

"Are those real islands?" asked the young prince.

---

[81] *Ibid.*, pages #550-2.

"Of course they are real islands," said the man in evening dress.

"And those strange and troubling creatures?"

"They are all genuine and authentic princesses."

"Then God also must exist!" cried the prince.

"I am God," replied the man in full evening dress, with a bow.

The young prince returned home as quickly as he could.

"So you are back," said his father, the king.

"I have seen islands, I have seen princesses, I have seen God," said the prince reproachfully.

The king was unmoved.

"Neither real islands, nor real princesses, nor a real God, exist."

"I saw them!"

"Tell me how God was dressed."

"God was in full evening dress."

"Were the sleeves of his coat rolled back?"

The prince remembered that they had been. The king smiled.

"That is the uniform of a magician. You have been deceived."

At this, the prince returned to the next land, and went to the same shore, where once again he came upon the man in full evening dress.

"My father the king has told me who you are," said the young prince indignantly. "You deceived me last time, but not again. Now I know that those are not real islands and real princesses, because you are a magician."

The man on the shore smiled.

"It is you who are deceived, my boy. In your father's kingdom there are many islands and many princesses. But you are under your father's spell, so you cannot see them."

The prince returned pensively home. When he saw his father, he looked him in the eyes.

"Father, is it true that you are not a real king, but only a magician?"

The king smiled, and rolled back his sleeves.

"Yes, my son, I am only a magician."

"Then the man on the shore was God."

"The man on the shore was another magician."

"I must know the real truth, the truth beyond magic."

"There is no truth beyond magic," said the king.

The prince was full of sadness.

He said, "I will kill myself."

The king by magic caused death to appear. Death stood in the door and beckoned to the prince. The prince shuddered. He remembered the beautiful but unreal islands and the unreal but beautiful princesses.

"Very well," he said. "I can bear it."

"You see, my son," said the king, "you too now begin to be a magician."

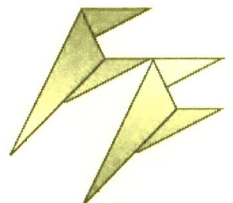

Bibliography

The Bibliography for *FindFar* is identical to that of *MindWar*, as the MW principles and technologies are applied as pertinent herein. For the detailed discussions to which all of the listed publications refer, please see *MindWar* itself.

Alexander, Lt. Colonel John B., "The New Mental Battlefield: 'Beam Me Up, Spock'". Leavenworth: U.S. Army Command & General Staff College *Military Review*, December 1980.

Andersen, Per & Andersson, Sven Anders, *Physiological Basis of the Alpha Rhythm*. New York: Appleton-Century Crofts, 1968.

Anderson, William Henry, "Terrorism: The Underlying Causes", *The Intelligencer*. Washington, D.C.: Association of Former Intelligence Officers, 2004.

Anneman, Theodore, *Practical Mental Effects*. New York: Tannen Magic, 1963.

Aquinas, Thomas, *Summa Theologica*. New York: Benziger Brothers, Inc, 1911 (English), 1948.

Aquino, Lt. Colonel Michael A., Barony of Rachane: *MindStar*. 2016.
MindWar. 2013, 2016.
"Psychological Operations: The Ethical Dimension." Washington, D.C.: National Defense University, 1987.

Ardrey, Robert, *The Social Contract*. New York: Atheneum, 1970.

Army, Department of the, Field Manuals: Washington, D.C.:
3-05.301, *Psychological Operations Process: Tactics, Techniques, and Procedures*, 30 August 2007.
3-53, *Military Information Support Operations*, January 2013.
33-1, *Psychological Operations*, 3 August 1979.
90-2, *Battlefield Deception*, 3 October 1988.

Asimov, Isaac, [in narrative sequence] New York: Doubleday,
Prelude to Foundation. 1988.
Forward the Foundation. 1993.
Foundation. 1951.
Foundation and Empire. 1952.
Second Foundation, 1953.

Foundation's Edge. 1981.

Foundation and Earth. 1986.

Atkinson, William W., *The Will: Its Nature, Power, and Development.* London: L.N. Fowler & Co., 1915.

Aurelius, Marcus, *Meditations.* New York: Penguin Books, 1964.

Becker, Robert O. and Selden, Gary, *The Body Electric: Electromagnetism and the Foundation of Life.* New York: William Morrow, 1985.

Belashchenkow, T., "'Black Propaganda' From Fort Bragg". Moscow: *Sovetskiy Voin,* 1980.

Bloom, Howard, *The Lucifer Principle: A Scientific Expedition into the Policies of History.* New York: Atlantic Monthly Press, 1995.

Burr, Harold Saxon, *The Fields of Life: Our Links with the Universe.* New York: Ballantine Books, 1972.

Camus, Albert, *Resistance, Rebellion, and Death: Essays.* New York: Alfred A. Knopf, 1960.

Carradine, David, *The Spirit of Shaolin.* Boston: Charles E. Tuttle, 1991.

Carrol, Noel, *The Philosophy of Horror, or Paradoxes of the Heart.* New York: Routledge, 1990.

Chandler, Robert W., *War of Ideas: The U.S. Propaganda Campaign in Vietnam.* Boulder: Westview Press, 1981.

Chayefsky, Paddy, *Altered States.* New York: Harper Collins, 1978.

Cleary, Thomas (Trans.), *The Secret of the Golden Flower.* San Francisco: HarperSanFrancisco, 1991.

Combs, James E. & Nimmo, Dan, *A Primer of Politics.* New York: Macmillan Publishing Co., 1984.

Corinda, *Thirteen Steps to Mentalism.* New York: Louis Tannen, 1967.

Cornish, Edward, *Futuring: The Exploration of the Future.* Bethesda: World Future Society, 2004.

Cowie, Peter, *The Apocalypse Now Book*. Cambridge: Da Capo Press, 2000.

Davis, Wade E., *The Serpent and the Rainbow*. New York: Warner Books, 1987.

Dawkins, Richard, *The Selfish Gene*. New York: Oxford University Press, 1989.

de Lafforest, Roger, *Houses That Kill*. Paris: Robert Laffont, 1972.

Deibel, Terry L., *Foreign Affairs Strategy: Logic for American Statecraft*. New York: Cambridge University Press, 2007.

Delgado, José M.R., *Physical Control of the Mind: Towards a Psychocivilized Society*. New York: Harper & Row, 1969.

Drezner, Daniel W., *Theories of International Politics and Zombies*. Princeton: Princeton University Press, 2011.

Dunlop, Beth, *Building a Dream: The Art of Disney Architecture*. New York: Harry N. Abrams, 1996.

Edwardes, Michael, *The Dark Side of History: Magic in the Making of Man*. New York: Stein & Day, 1977.

Elliot, Andrew J. & Aarts, Henk, "Perception of the Color Red Enhances the Force and Velocity of Motor Output". *Emotion*, Vol 11(2), April 2011.

Eisenberg, David & Wright, Thomas Lee, *Encounters with Qi: Exploring Chinese Medicine*. New York: W.W. Norton, 1995.

Eisner, Lotte H., *The Haunted Screen*. Berkeley: University of California Press, 1965.

Ellul, Jacques, *Propaganda: The Formation of Men's Attitudes*. New York: Vintage Books, 1973.

Ferguson, Marilyn, *The Brain Revolution*. New York: Bantam Books, 1975.

Fisher, Roger, William L. Ury, & Bruce Patton, *Getting to Yes: Negotiating Agreement Without Giving In*. New York: Penguin Books, 1983.

Fleming, Ian, *Casino Royale*. New York: The Macmillan Company, 1953.

Fowles, John, Boston: Little, Brown & Company,
The Áristos. 1964.
The Magus. 1965.

Gerring, John, *Social Science Methodology: A Unified Framework* (2nd Edition). New York: Cambridge University Press, 2012.

Green, Ronald E., *The Persuasive Properties of Color*. Marketing Communications, October 1984.

Grosser, Maurice, *The Painter's Eye*. New York: Rinehart & Co., 1956.

Gykha, Matila, *The Geometry of Art and Life*. New York: Dover Publications, 1977.

Hall, Edward T., *The Hidden Dimension*. Garden City: Doubleday & Co., 1966.

Hatsumi, Masaaki, *The Way of the Ninja: Secret Techniques*. Tokyo: Kodansha International, 2004.

Hersey, G.L., *Pythagorean Palaces: Magic and Architecture in the Italian Renaissance*. Ithaca: Cornell University Press, 1976.

Herzog, Arthur, *The B.S. Factor: The Theory and Technique of Faking It in America*. New York: Simon & Schuster, 1973.

Hitler, Adolf, *Mein Kampf*. (Michael Ford Trans.) Munich: Verlag Franz Eher, 1935.

Hoban, Jack E., *The Ethical Warrior*. Spring Lake: RGI Media, 2012.

Hoffer, Eric, *The True Believer*. New York: Harper & Row, 1951.

Hudson, Valerie M., Schrodt, Philip A., & Whitmer, Ray D., *A New Kind of Social Science: The Path Beyond Current (IR) Methodologies May Lie Beneath Them*. Montreal: International Studies Association, March 26, 2004.

Huntley, H.E., *The Divine Proportion: A Study in Mathematical Beauty*. New York: Dover Publications, 1970.

Iacoboni, Marco, Roger P. Woods, Marcel Brass, Harold Bekkering, John C. Mazziotta, Giacomo Rizzolatti, "Cortical Mechanisms of Human Imitation", *Science* Magazine, December 24, 1999.

The Imagineers, *Walt Disney Imagineering: A Behind the Dreams Look at Making the Magic Real*. New York: Hyperion, 1996.

Iyer, Raghavan N., New York: Oxford University Press, *The Moral and Political Thought of Mahatma Gandhi*. 1973.
ParaPolitics: Toward the City of Man. 1979.

Jaspers, Karl, *Nietzsche*. Tucson: University of Arizona Press, 19065

Kantner, Paul, *Planet Earth Rock and Roll Orchestra*. San Francisco: Little Dragon Publishing Company, 1983.

Kccl, John A., *The Eighth Tower*. New York: E.P. Dutton & Co., 1975.

Kissin, Benjamin, "Conscious and Unconscious Programs in the Brain" (*Psychobiology of Human Behavior*, Volume 1). New York: Plenum Medical Books, 1986.

Konner, Melvin, *The Tangled Web: Biological Constraints on the Human Spirit*. New York: Holt, Rinehart & Winston, 1982.

Kripal, Jeffrey J.,
Esalen. Chicago: University of Chicago Press, 2007.
(Ed. with Glenn W. Shuck) *On the Edge of the Future*. Bloomington: Indiana University Press, 2005.

Kurtz, Rudolf, *Expressionismus und Film*. Zürich: Chronos Verlag, 1926.

Lee, Bruce, *Tao of Jeet Kune Do*. Burbank: Ohara Publications, 1975.

Lee, Martin A. & Shlain, Bruce, *Acid Dreams: The Complete Social History of LSD: The CIA, the Sixties, and Beyond* (Revised Edition). New York: Grove Press, 1994.

Lemezma, Marc, London: New Holland Publishers:
Mind Magic. 2003.
Mind Tricks. 2007.

Lilly, John C., *The Deep Self*. New York: Warner Books, 1977.

London, Perry, *Behavior Control*. New York: Harper & Row, 1969.

Luce, Gay Gaer, *Body Time*. New York: Bantam Books, 1971.

Machiavelli, Niccolò, *The Prince and The Discourses*. New York: Random House, 1950.

Mackay, Charles, *Extraordinary Popular Delusions and the Madness of Crowds*. New York: Harmony Books, 1980 (reprint 1841).

Mandelbaum, Adam, *The Psychic Battlefield: A History of the Military-Occult Complex*. New York: St. Martin's Press, 2000.

Marks, John, *The Search for the "Manchurian Candidate": The CIA and Mind Control*. New York: New York Times Books, 1979.

McRae, Ron, *Mind Wars*. New York: St. Martin's Press, 1984.

Mlodinow, Leonard, *Subliminal: How Your Unconscious Mind Rules Your Behavior*. New York: Pantheon, 2012.

Mortensen, William, *The Command to Look: A Formula for Picture Success*. San Francisco: Camera Craft Publishing Company, 1937.

Murphy, Michael,
An End to Ordinary History. Los Angeles: J.P. Tarcher, 1982.
Jacob Atabet. Millbrae: Celestial Arts, 1977.

Naselaris, Thomas *et al.*, "Bayesian Reconstruction of Natural Images from Human Brain Activity", *Neuron 63*, September 24, 2009.

Nashel, Jonathan, *Edward Lansdale's Cold War*. Amherst: University of Massachusetts Press, 2005.

Orwell, George, *1984*. New York: Harcourt, Brace & Co., 1949.

Oschman, James L., *Energy Medicine: The Scientific Basis*. New York: Churchhill Livingstone, 2000.

Ouspensky, Peter D., *The Psychology of Man's Possible Evolution*. New York: Alfred A. Knopf, 1969.

Penrose, Roger, *Shadows of the Mind: A Search for the Missing Science of Consciousness*. Oxford: Oxford University Press, 1994.

Plato, *The Collected Dialogues of Plato* (Ed. Edith Hamilton & Huntington Cairns). Princeton: Princeton University Press, 1961.

Playfair, Guy and Hill, Scott, *The Cycles of Heaven: Cosmic Forces and What They are Doing to You*. London: Souvenir Press, 1978.

Pollock, Daniel C. (Project Director), *The Art and Science of Psychological Operations: Case Studies of Military Application* (2 volumes). Washington, D.C. Department of the Army, 1972.

Prouty, L. Fletcher, *JFK: The CIA, Vietnam, and the Plot to Assassinate John F. Kennedy*. New York: Carol Publishing Group, 1996.

Randi, James, *Flim-Flam: Psychics, ESP, Unicorns, and Other Delusions*. Buffalo: Prometheus Books, 1982.

Reed, Graham, *The Psychology of Anomalous Experience*. Boston: Houghton Mifflin, 1974.

Roenneberg, Till, *Internal Time: Chronotypes, Social Jet Lag, and Why You're So Tired*. Cambridge: Harvard University Press, 2012.

Roetter, Charles, *Psychological Warfare*. London: B.T. Batsford Ltd, 1974.

Ronson, Jon, *The Men Who Stare At Goats*. New York: Simon & Schuster, 2004.

Russell, Edward W., *Design for Destiny*. New York: Ballantine Books, 1971.

Schneider, Al, *The Theory and Practice of Magic Deception*. Amazon.com: CreateSpace, 2011.

Seese, Major Gregory S., "Science of Influence: A Primer for Psychological Operations". Fort Bragg, N.C.: John F. Kennedy Special Warfare Center & School, 2013.

Sibley, Mulford Q., *Political Ideas and Ideologies: A History of Political Thought*. New York: Harper & Row, 1970.

Somit, Albert, *Political Science and the Study of the Future*. Hinsdale: The Dryden Press, 1974.

Soyka, Fred & Edmonds, Alan, *The Ion Effect*. New York: E.P. Dutton, 1977.

Subcommittee on Health and Scientific Research of the Committee on Human Resources, U.S. Congress, "Human Drug Testing by the CIA, 1977". Washington, D.C.: *Congressional Record*, September 20, 1977.

Taylor, Philip M., *Munitions of the Mind*. Manchester: Manchester University Press, 2003.

Thomas, Donald, *The Marquis de Sade*. Boston: New York Graphic Society, 1976.

Trafton, Anne, "Moral Judgments Can Be Altered By Magnets". Cambridge: *MIT News*, March 30, 2010.

Travers, P.L., *Mary Poppins*. Boston: Houghton Mifflin Harcourt, 1934.

Tzu, Lao, *Tao Te Ching* (Stephen Mitchell Trans.). London: Frances Lincoln, 2009.

Ury, William L., *Getting Past No: Negotiating in Difficult Situations*. New York: Bantam Books, 1993.

Vallely, Colonel Paul E., with Aquino, Major Michael A., "From PSYOP to MindWar: The Psychology of Victory". San Francisco: 7th Psychological Operations Group, 1980.

Vandewalle, G., C. Schmidt, G. Albouy, V. Sterpenich, A. Darsaud, G. Rauchs, P.-Y. Berken, E. Balteau, C. Degueldre, A. Luxen, P. Maquet, D.J. Dijk, "Brain Responses to Violet, Blue, and Green Monochromatic Light Exposures in Humans : Prominent Role of Blue Light and the Brainstem". *PLoS One*, 11/28/2007.

Veith, Liza (Trans), *The Yellow Emperor's Classic of Internal Medicine*. Berkeley: University of California Press, 2002.

Verne, Jules, New York:
    Journey to the Center of the Earth. Signet Classics, 2012.
    20,000 Leagues Under the Sea ("The Annotated Jules Verne" by Walter James Miller). Thomas Y. Crowell, 1976.

Viereck, Peter, *Metapolitics from the Romantics to Hitler*. New York: Alfred A. Knopf, 1941.

von Harbou, Thea, *Metropolis*. Germany, 1927.

Walker, Morton, *The Power of Color*; Avery Publishing Group, 1991.

Washnis, George J. & Hricak, R.Z., *Discovery of Magnetic Health*. Rockville, MD: Nova Publishing Company, 1993.

Waters, T.A., *Mind, Myth, and Magic*. Seattle: Hermetic Press, 1993.

White, John (Ed.), *Psychic Warfare: Fact or Fiction?* Wellingborough: The Aquarian Press, 1988.

Whitrow, G.J., *The Nature of Time*. New York: Oxford University Press, 1972.

Winkler, Franz E., *For Freedom Destined: Mysteries of Man's Evolution in the Mythology of Wagner's Ring Operas and Parsifal*. Garden City: Waldorf Press, 1974.

Index

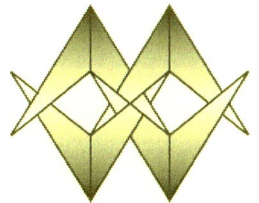

Accessories

For MindWar accessories
please feel welcome to visit:

http://www.zazzle.com/mindwar

... for a gradually-increasing selection of MindWar,
MindWar Branch, MetaForce Branch, and
ParaPolitics Branch raiment and memorabilia.

About the Author

After commencing his military career as Cadet Colonel of the Santa Barbara High School Jr. ROTC in 1964, Michael Aquino was commissioned in the Regular Army as a Sr. ROTC Distinguished Military Graduate of the University of California in 1968. After a year with the 1/17th Cavalry, 82nd Airborne Division, he completed the PSYOP Officer Course at the John F. Kennedy Special Warfare School, in which he was among select students cross-trained with the concurrent Special Forces Officer Course.

During 1969-70 he was assigned to the 6th PSYOP Battalion, 4th Group, Vietnam. As an HA Command & Control Team Leader, he was responsible for both tactical (HB) teams in combat operations, and audio-visual (HE) teams in the Civil Operations & Revolutionary Development Support (CORDS) program, and flew numerous PSYOP air support missions throughout III Corps Tactical Zone with both the U.S. Air Force and Army aviation.

In 1972 he joined the 306th PSYOP Battalion (Strategic), USAR at Fort MacArthur, California, and for the next seven years served as Research & Analysis (FA) Team Leader, Operations Officer, and finally Executive Officer. In the 306th - whose members ranged from eccentric Hollywood personalities to dour L.A.P.D. officers - he oversaw highly-classified Basic PSYOP Studies for the Joint Chiefs of Staff, PSYOP support for the training of units such as the 12th Special Forces, and use of the 306th's atmospheric World War II-era bunkers for space combat scenes in the original *Battlestar Galactica* television series.

In 1976 he was selected for the Foreign Area Officer career program, completed that qualification at the Special Warfare Center and Central Intelligence Agency during the next three years, and participated in NATO REFORGER exercises as a Western Europe specialist. In 1976 he also completed the remaining course requirements for Special Forces, and was awarded that Tab upon its creation in 1984.

From 1979 to 1981 he served as the FA Team Leader for Headquarters, 7th PSYOP Group in San Francisco, during which time he and the Group Commander collaborated on the predecessor concept paper to this *MindWar* book.

Returning to active duty in 1981, he was transferred to Civil Affairs Branch, completed its Advanced Course at the Special Warfare Center as the Distinguished Graduate, and received the rare Primary Skill identifier of Politico-Military Affairs Officer (48G). In this capacity he was sent to the State Department Foreign Service Institute and the Defense Intelligence Agency for Attaché qualification, completed the Military Intelligence Officer Advanced Course at Fort

Huachuca, and in 1986 was reassigned to Military Intelligence Branch.

In 1986-7 he was the sole USAR officer selected to attend the Industrial College of the National Defense University. During that year he worked with the U.S. Information Agency representative at the National War College on the *PSYOP Ethics* paper which is also a predecessor to this book.

In 1990 as one of the Army's first officers to be certified in Joint Space Intelligence by the U.S. Air Force, he was assigned to J2 HQ U.S. Space Command, where in Section X, out of the Cheyenne Mountain NORAD complex, he was involved with those files until he retired from the Active USAR in 1994.

Since the Army had waited until the exact date of his final USA retirement 2006 to create the PSYOP Branch, it graciously transferred him "posthumously" to the Green & Grey in 2011. He has retained his original affiliation with the 1st Special Forces Regiment out of respect for that unique honor.

American decorations include the Bronze Star, Meritorious Service Medal, Air Medal, three Army Commendation Medals, two Army Reserve Achievement Medals, Parachutist Badge, Special Forces Tab, and USAF Space & Missile Badge. Vietnamese decorations include the Gallantry Cross, Psychological Warfare Medal, and Air Service Medal.

Academically he received the Ph.D. in Political Science from the University of California in 1980 and the M.P.A. in National Resource Management from George Washington University in 1987. He taught as Adjunct Professor of Political Science at Golden Gate University 1980-86.

Professionally he is a member of the Special Forces, PSYOP, Civil Affairs, Former Intelligence Officers, and Air/Space/Missile Defense Associations.

He is a past National Commander of the Knights of Dunamis (Eagle Scout Honor Society) and recipient of its Knight Eagle Distinguished Service Award. He has also received the Vigil Honor of Scouting's Order of the Arrow, and the Distinguished Service Key of Alpha Phi Omega Fraternity.

He is a Priest of the ancient Egyptian god Set.

After the conclusion of his U.S. government service, the Constitution permitted him to be recognized by Scotland's Lord Lyon King of Arms as the current Baron of Rachane, Argyllshire. He, Baroness Lilith, and inevitable, immortal cats live in San Francisco.